I, NADIA,
WIFE OF A
TERRORIST

France Overseas:
*Studies in Empire
and Decolonization*

SERIES EDITORS:
Philip Boucher,
A. J. B. Johnston,
James D. Le Sueur,
and Tyler Stovall

I, NADIA, WIFE OF A TERRORIST

BAYA GACEMI

with a foreword by Fanny Colonna

and an introductory essay by Edmund Burke III

Translated by Paul Côté and Constantina Mitchell

University of Nebraska Press | Lincoln and London

Publication of this book was assisted by a grant from the
National Endowment for the Arts.

NATIONAL
ENDOWMENT
FOR THE ARTS

Cet ouvrage publié dans le cadre du programme d'aide à
la publication bénéficie du soutien du Ministère des Af-
faires Etrangères et du Service Culturel de l'Ambassade de
France représenté aux Etats-Unis.

This work, published as part of the program of aid for
publication, received support from the French Ministry
of Foreign Affairs and the Cultural Service of the French
Embassy in the United States.

Library of Congress Cataloging-in-Publication Data
Nadia, 1975 or 6-
[Moi, Nadia, femme d'un émir du GIA. English]
I, Nadia, wife of a terrorist / Baya Gacemi ; translated
by Paul Côté and Constantina Mitchell.
p. cm. — (France overseas)
ISBN-13: 978-0-8032-2204-5 (cloth : alk. paper)
ISBN-10: 0-8032-2204-1 (cloth : alk. paper)
ISBN-13: 978-0-8032-7124-1 (pbk. : alk. paper)
ISBN-10: 0-8032-7124-7 (pbk. : alk. paper)
1. Nadia, 1975 or 6-   2. Women political
activists — Algeria — Biography.   I. Gacemi,
Baya.   II. Title.   III. Series.
DT295.652.N33A3 2006
965.05092–dc22
2005046657

Set in Garamond by Kim Essman.
Designed by A. Shahan.

CONTENTS

FOREWORD

Fanny Colonna

Despite its modest appearance, *I, Nadia, Wife of a Terrorist* is essential for understanding the violent struggle that tore Algeria apart between 1992 and 2002. Yet were it not for the determination of the Algerian journalist Baya Gacemi and the involvement of a local support group for victims of the violence, this book would not exist. Indeed, were it not for the locally denigrated Algerian state television, Nadia would not have learned of the existence of the support group. This group is but one example among many of the remarkable effectiveness of Algerian women's groups in their various struggles. However, let's be clear: This book is not mostly about the violence inflicted on women during this period by the various armed groups (those of the state and the Islamists) or even about the violence of ordinary men upon ordinary women. Nor, finally, is it about women's resistance to that violence.

Paradoxically, this book is primarily about the *seduction* that the Islamist program and the ensuing selective and endemic violence exercised for a time, especially upon those most at risk—women of rural or semi-urban background, inadequately educated and grossly unprepared for adult life. As a result of the events of 1989 in particular, as well as the atmosphere of the post-one-party state more generally, they had been awakened to expect a better life and a personal destiny. Even older women who had experienced the 1954–62 revolution in all its horrors and its broken promises and who might have been expected to have more sense proved susceptible to the Islamist message.

The Algerian women's movement, to speak only of independent (post-1962) Algeria, had been in the avant-garde of the social struggle. Its first great public assembly dates from 1979, a year after the death of President Houari Boumedienne (December 1978) and a year before the Kabyle Berber spring uprising (Spring 1980). The assembly took place in a prestigious space, the main lecture hall in central Algiers, where doctoral theses are defended. Those in attendance spoke without restraint. Certainly no Islamist woman sought to speak.

However, this audacious initiative failed to prevent the imposition five years later of a regressive Family Code profoundly inspired by the *shari'ah* (Muslim religious law). It also failed to prevent the arrest of many members of the Algerian women's associations created following the 1979 assembly, including a woman who was pregnant at the time. Unfortunately, while these women's incarceration was short—less than one month—the 1984 Family Code is still law in Algeria. Nadia and the women like her who joined, supported, or at least did not disavow the armed Islamist groups until their final bloody excesses would probably have heard of these groups. They would almost certainly have known of the important gatherings of Islamist women beginning in 1989, which were organized under the aegis of the Islamic Salvation Front (known by its acronym, the FIS).

Women played an important role in the Algerian revolutionary struggle, a fact immortalized by the film *The Battle of Algiers*. The Algerian revolution produced many heroines, and a few streets even bear their names. However, it is worth mentioning that no female political leader emerged on the national level then or earlier (1920–54), when nationalism had begun to emerge. Finally, we might also note that contrary to the situation in Egypt and Pakistan, the Algerian Islamist movement failed to produce any theorists or even theologians of note. Prominent female intellectuals and artists did not publicly convert to Islamism, as occurred in Egypt and Turkey. Algeria is thus a bipolar society—the extremes rarely come together. How can we explain this? Algerian women who joined the national movement with "their men" seemed to be guided only by masculine models and masculine political discourse. Thus their political involvement appears to us as a kind of "mobilization of closeness," which is not to say that they were illegitimate or lacking in critical distance and sincerity in their willingness to oppose the state (colonial, and later, national).

In the past twenty to thirty years—depending on how one counts—Algeria has not only failed to maintain the status quo but has gone backward with respect to women's legal rights, and this has affected all social groups (not just the poor). If we read Nadia's account attentively, we find in addition to her story the portraits of ten or a dozen other women, Houria, Hadda, Fatma, Khadija, Fahla (the valiant), Djouher, and others, whose names aren't mentioned: schoolgirls, a dining hall worker, the wife of a terrorist, the widow of a terrorist, the mother of a rebel, and lovers, mothers, or married women of conviction sometimes acting against the wishes of their husbands. Now we can use the past tense to write about the Algeria that Nadia describes, and we can see that the Islamist project of social transformation was defeated by force even as it destroyed itself by its own excesses. This should make us think again about women's capacities for civility and peace, if one ever had the slightest illusion about the subject.

Nadia's story illuminates the very special, as well as characteristic, context of the Algeria in which she lived. This is true in terms of both the geography and the chronology in which it unfolds. The geography was characterized by very recently established villages that were poorly equipped, more or less "socialist," and had been constructed for agricultural workers around the edges of the state-owned farms (which were themselves created from the expropriated prosperous former colonial estates). This land was inhabited by people who had come from the mountains of the hinterland in the nineteenth century and who had preserved close connections with their strongly tribal culture even while they themselves were surrounded by colonial settlements. Workers and employees of the state farms moved depending on where there was work and housing within this impoverished space, while their identities and solidarities (those of the family) were both limited and precarious. This was just the situation of Nadia's family. They lacked a real connection both to employment and to a space in which they had socially and emotionally invested. This situation was also the tragedy of Nadia's father and the source of Nadia's difficulties: she was not at home anywhere because her family had no place to call its own. Chronologically, it was during this period that the level if not the quality of education rapidly increased and many schools were constructed. For the first time, girls began to want to attend school—although the family, and especially the mothers, of these girls were much less persuaded of its importance. Nadia had the best and the worst of this situation, and the sharp contrast helps explain why she so desperately wanted to get married at such a young age and why she initially experienced being married as a great adventure.

This said, we need to recognize that a particular feminine sensibility, not to mention women's support for the Islamists, was not due only to a woman's proximity to Algiers, the capital. Many other conditions—for example, the forced sedentarization of nomadic groups, the collapse of "socialist villages" after the withdrawal of state support, and the existence of suburban towns with no work or leisure activities—in other places could have provoked similarly anomic situations. But all sorts of contradictory interpretations about the origins of Islamism among men (and women) in Algeria have flourished. Given this state of sociological indeterminacy, we must wonder whether completely opposite conditions—involving confident, if not satisfied, people—might not have produced similar outcomes; of course, we have no real situation to which to make comparisons.

In the early 1990s, the Algerian Islamist groups gradually developed an underground movement, much as all guerrilla movements against occupiers had done, including resisters to Nazi rule in occupied Europe. H. R. Kedward, a British historian of the French resistance movement during the Second World War, has suggested that one reason why we know so little about these struggles and their secret violence is because we know almost nothing about the role of women. As this book demonstrates, Kedward's hypothesis seems to work for the Algerian Islamist struggle between 1993 and 1996, although the legacy of the revolution of 1954–62, which accorded a high symbolic status to the guerrilla struggle, no doubt also played a determining role. Finally, the Islamists' adopting a strategy of guerrilla warfare derived as well from the proximity of the mountains of Kabilya to the Mitidja Plain, which provides a good place to hide from the authorities. It is in this zone that Nadia lived with her parents.

For these reasons, Nadia's story cannot be read only as a social document, even if it is as informative it is disconcerting, and as accurate in recording her experience, if not true in every sense. The book is based upon a lengthy taped interview, although some details and segments of the narrative appear to have been noted and incorporated only later, during the writing process. Although this book takes the form of a love story, it is also something rather different: the story of a rebellion, of the refusal of a young peasant girl to accept a wife's lot, the destiny of an Algerian woman in this particular time and place. It tells how a poor adolescent girl tried every means in this terrible time to avoid her fate. Nadia is a rebel when she harshly judges her father, when she mockingly debates her husband—the assassin—when she stands up to the police and doesn't let them have the last word so as not to betray not so much her husband as the cause to which she had given herself. In so doing, she remains faithful to herself. But her rebellion is not only that of an individual. Her story resembles that of the ten women whom we meet in the course of reading the book, and all the others like her, who completely refuse to accept their plight as scripted by others.

On January 10, 2005, Amnesty International issued a briefing to the UN Committee on the Elimination of Discrimination Against Women, on the failure of the Algerian government to protect women from rape, violence, and legal and economic discrimination. The report also chastised the government for failing to investigate and bring to justice those responsible for thousands of "disappearances" during the 1990s conflict. (A copy of the briefing can be found online at http://amnesty-news.c.topica.com/maac3zKabdbxcbbohoZb).

NADIA AND AHMED

AN ALGERIAN TRAGEDY

Edmund Burke III

Americans are perplexed by the appeal of Islamism. More disturbing still perhaps is the fact that Islamism has proved attractive to many Muslim women. Why have some become Islamist extremists, even at the risk of their lives (and the lives of their families)? Baya Gacemi's portrait of Nadia, a young Algerian woman, and her Islamist husband, Ahmed, depicts just such a person. The book is set in Algeria, where for some years, beginning in 1992, a dirty war has pitted "the state" against a variety of Islamist groups. (As readers will see, things are almost never what they seem in Algeria.) Based upon the life of Nadia, a young Algerian girl, as told to Baya Gacemi, an Algerian female journalist, this book is one of the few first-person accounts we have of the process by which a young woman became an Islamist extremist—and lived to tell the tale.

As the book begins, Nadia is a sixteen-year-old Algerian girl from "Hai Bounab," a small town in the Mitidja plain south of Algiers, the capital. (Both her name and that of the village are pseudonyms, because the violence that affects Algeria continues at the time of writing.) Against the better judgment of her parents, young Nadia marries Ahmed Chaabani, a local hooligan whose rebel spirit she finds irresistible. Alas, in the first of a series of personal transformations, even before the marriage, Ahmed has moved from committing petty crimes to becoming a foot soldier in and subsequently the local emir (leader) of the Armed Islamic Group, known by its acronym GIA. Before marrying Ahmed, Nadia leaves school and gives up on the prospect of a better life. Marrying Ahmed, she is plunged headlong into a nightmare that lasts more than four years.

At first the young wife of the Islamist hit man enjoys being called "the Mother of the Believers." But as den mother to Ahmed and his gang she is quickly forced to conform to the strictest Islamist code while remaining on call to minister to their needs around the clock. By 1996 the police are hunting for her and her husband. Heavily pregnant and in the depths of an Algerian winter, she hits bottom. Her parents are terrified of being associated with her and so put her and her new baby out of the house. By now a virtual outcast in Hai Bounab, she is reviled by her relatives and threatened with death by her neighbors as the polarization between the Islamists and the local government increases, stretching her life to the breaking point.

Nadia's story brings us face to face with the roots of terrorism. It exposes a nightmarish patriarchal struggle that mars the lives of countless rural Algerian women, and it explains why some of them went to such lengths to support the GIA. Baya Gacemi's book also helps us understand the connections between Nadia's personal rebellion and the larger Islamist upheaval against the Algerian authorities (which despite its duration and savagery remains little known to Americans). Gacemi's book lends a human face to the Algerian tragedy.

The story of what happened in Hai Bounab takes us into the heart of the darkness that has been Algeria since 1992. After independence in 1962 Hai Bounab became one of the self-managed peasant socialist villages established on former French settler lands. For a time it enjoyed the benefits of the socialist experiment. By the 1990s, however, socialist agriculture had become passé, and the state turned to the dynamic petroleum sector to keep the economy moving. Villages like Hai Bounab, chronically underfunded and mismanaged, were virtually abandoned by the state. All too aware of their dead-end status, the villagers increasingly resented a government they came to regard sarcastically as "*le pouvoir*" ("the power"). This resentment offered fertile soil to oppositionists, and the Islamists were quick to take advantage.

How did things come to such a pass? The story Baya Gacemi recounts is complex enough to benefit from further contextualization.

Beginning with the French conquest in 1830, modern Algerian history has been marked by a prolonged and bitter struggle over land, pitting French settlers against Algerian peasants in a brutal conflict. One hundred and thirty-two years of French rule drastically weakened Algerian Islam, especially the Islam of the urban *ulama* (clergy), even as it further empowered the rural marabouts (or Sufi holy men), many of whom agreed to collaborate with the French. This legacy of collaboration, together with a deliberate French policy of de-Islamization helped ensure that nationalism, when it finally emerged after World War II, would be predominantly secular. (We catch a glimpse of this complex reality in the 1966 Gillo Pontecorvo film *The Battle of Algiers*.)

The Algerian revolutionary struggle (1954–62) mobilized rural populations against the French colonial authorities and the settlers. Yet it was simultaneously a civil war that left a bitter legacy of violence and factional politics. Almost a million Algerian men and women perished in this eight-year struggle, while hundreds of thousands of others were brutally tortured and psychologically maimed. This legacy of violence continues to haunt the society, springing to life in surprising ways, as the story of Nadia demonstrates.

The independence struggle mobilized large numbers of Algerian women as messengers, medics, and behind-the-lines supporters. Some even transported and planted bombs (as dramatized in *The Battle of Algiers*). Women likewise endured torture at the hands of the French, who employed it systematically against both sexes (vigorously denying it all the while). Given the scale of women's sacrifices, one might expect that they played a large political role in independent Algeria. After the shooting stopped, however, the heroines of the revolution were pushed to one side. Few entered the government and few streets were named after them. Gacemi's book assumes readers know this history.

The first decades after Algerian independence were dramatic and surprising. Despite a galloping birth rate, the absence of trained professionals, and a badly splintered elite, Algeria emerged in the 1970s as a model socialist agricultural society with a booming petroleum sector. Algerian diplomats extolled the benefits of Third Worldism (the idea that a middle way existed between U.S. capitalism and Soviet communism). Frantz Fanon's *Wretched of the Earth* provides a glimpse into the revolution's utopianism as well as its violence. But by the time of President Boumedienne's death in 1978, the dreams that had once animated the Algerian leadership had dissipated, and Algeria's state-led development model was in crisis.

The presidency of Boumedienne's successor, Chadli Bendjedid (1979–92) coincided with the cold war's end (the Soviet Union had been a key ally) and corruption's reaching epic levels. It was also marked by neoliberal globalization. Although the state-led development strategy was in crisis everywhere (see, for example, Egypt and India), Algeria was hit especially hard in the 1980s. Algerian nationalism, formerly the bedrock of the state, imploded when its main institutions (the army, the Party of the National Liberation Front, and the national trade union—the UGTA) splintered and internecine struggles began. By the late 1980s a large underclass of semi-educated youths lacking jobs, housing, and education had emerged. In October 1988, riots in Algiers marked the arrival of political Islam on the national stage.

The events of October 1988 challenged the legitimacy of the governing regime and intensified the struggle among the many different factions, resulting in a major challenge to the establishment from the leading Islamist group, the Islamic Salvation

Front (FIS). It is important to note that the Islamists at first followed the path of legality in contesting the December 1991 parliamentary elections. The FIS and their allies won 188 of 232 seats outright, transforming the political scene. This victory also left the Islamists well placed to gain additional seats in the second round of the elections, which were scheduled for January 1992. In the interim, however, having suffered a massive electoral repudiation, the army intervened, canceling the elections, compelling President Benjedid to resign, legally dissolving the FIS, and arresting the FIS's leaders.

In retrospect, this bold stroke seems a catastrophic political miscalculation. The repression that followed drove the Islamists to take up arms and ignited a low-intensity civil war that continues at this writing. Over the next three years (1992–95) Algeria lived a nightmare of brutal massacres. (For example, in September 1997 the GIA massacred four hundred people in the village of Rais, fifteen kilometers from Algiers, and in January 1998 they killed two hundred at Bentalha (a village twenty kilometers east of Algiers). Government forces also committed atrocities (about which Gacemi does not speak). To date, more than thirty thousand Algerians (some would put the total much higher) have been killed, including hundreds of journalists and intellectuals. Nadia's biography dramatically depicts just how high this cost has been.

The Algerian journalist Baya Gacemi's portrait of Nadia must therefore be understood as a work of courage. Gacemi interviewed Nadia at length in February 1997. They met in a time of bitter and protracted conflict in their country. Gacemi's book, *Moi, Nadia, Femme d'un Emir du GIA*, published in 1998 by Seuil, a leading Parisian publishing house, created a sensation in France. The book describes a dizzying descent into madness and fear. American readers need to hear Nadia's story too.

I, NADIA,
WIFE OF A
TERRORIST

INTRODUCTION

I first met Nadia (that's what we'll call her) at the headquarters of the "El Azhar" Association run by one of my friends, Dalila Allal. I was doing a news story on women victimized by terrorism. Nadia was desperate. She had no money and needed help. She hadn't heard from her husband in a year and a half. Realizing he might never come back, she decided it was time to assume responsibility for herself. She was living with her parents, who constantly reminded her that she was a burden to them. They told her that as long as she stayed with them they, too, would be shunned by everyone and wouldn't even be able to return to their home. Nadia saw Dalila on TV and approached her for help in finding a place to stay so she could move out. Dalila took pity on Nadia, never passed judgment on her, and did what she could to be of assistance. She placed Nadia with a host family where she has remained to this day.

Nadia agreed to tell her story in this book—the story of her life with a local village "emir" in the Mitidja region of Algeria. Her husband, Ahmed, was the perfect example of a typical GIA (Armed Islamic Group) militant. Illiterate, uneducated, and accustomed to getting by any way he could, he was one of those social outcasts who looked to the GIA for status. And he believed he had attained it. Regardless of the means, what counted was that he had become a leader. People who used to dismiss him as little more than a smalltime hoodlum were now taking orders from him, because they, too, were convinced that things had changed forever. Like them, Nadia naively believed she was the master's wife, the "mother of the faithful." But the euphoria was short-lived, and Nadia soon found herself homeless, looking for shelter with each new day. Everybody rejected her, especially those who, just days before, had let her think that because she was the boss's wife she had reached the top. Her dreams of power and glory quickly vanished.

At the young age of twenty-two, Nadia willingly consented to share her experiences. She did so without embellishment or pretense, and even divulged details about her family and private life in the hope that her ordeal might serve as an example for other young women. The only condition she imposed on publishing this account was that the identity of those involved be concealed in order to protect her loved ones. She feels she has already caused them enough suffering. Consequently, every person's name has been changed. Some of the village names have been modified or transposed. The name of the rural community where the events transpired is purely fictitious. Nonetheless, I have ensured that the places mentioned in this book—and that really do exist—are identical in their geographical, sociological, and political configuration to those where the story actually unfolded.

One thing is incontestable: all the events recounted are factual and are presented as Nadia described them to me.

I know this book will have its detractors—at both ends of the spectrum.

There will most likely be some who think I give the security forces too much credit—an impression one could easily get reading this account. But nobody can deny that Nadia was lucky despite her misfortune. The local police chief took pity on her right from the start, viewing her more as a victim than a culprit. Still, that's not to imply that the way she was treated is necessarily the norm.

And there will be others who think the opposite: that I give the terrorists and their families too human a face and place too much blame on the patriots by accusing them of gratuitously executing terrorists' relatives. They might even be of the opinion that when a mother mourns the death of her terrorist sons, she's merely getting what she deserves for never having disassociated herself from their actions. Or they may not want to concede that an entire village could, at one point, have supported the GIA out of conviction. Instead, they'd rather harbor the outmoded populist notion that the common people are inherently good, and if they back the wrong cause, it's because they were forced to. The reality is often far more complex.

Since the onset of the violence in Algeria, emotions on both sides have hampered reasoned judgments and objective conclusions. Each faction takes it as given that the other is an enemy. Most analysts and politicians of note have taken cut-and-dried stands and provided nothing more than a blindly Manichaean assessment of the situation. Instead of quelling the resentment, which is what they should have done, they've poured oil on the fire. As for those who have taken pains to think things through logically before taking a stance, no one pays any attention to them. It's as plain as that.

Because of this simplistic approach, very few people, both in Algeria and beyond its borders, have really made an effort to understand the facts.

Baya Gacemi

My husband, Ahmed, died a month ago. He was killed during an operation led by the security forces in Chrea.[1] His body was recovered but they never found his head. The police assume his friends hid it after decapitating him. GIA terrorists are known to do that, especially in cases involving an "emir," like Ahmed, because it makes identification harder.[2] The police told my father they were sure it was Ahmed because they recognized the wound on his arm. I thought I had seen his body among several others on television one day, but the corpses they show look so similar it's hard to tell them apart.

I sensed his death was imminent. For some time before it happened, I'd sit in front of the TV every night at eight o'clock expecting to see his remains among those of the latest terrorists killed. My instincts were right. Two weeks ago the police from the Eucalyptus district, which includes the village of Hai Bounab, where Ahmed and I lived, informed my father of his death and asked him to relay the information to me. I immediately took my family record book to the police station, hoping they would update it by entering the change in my marital status.[3] Then I could go ahead and assume my new station in life: widow at twenty-two, and mother of an eighteen-month-old son. I'd been waiting for the news for such a long time. At last, I was going to be freed from the chains binding me to a man I hadn't seen since March of 1996 but whose existence weighed on me more with each passing day. The chief of police met with me and confirmed that he had received reports substantiating Ahmed's death: "Terrorists who were with him and taken alive have testified to the fact. But, by law, until the body has been positively identified, we can't assume he's dead, and we certainly can't state it on legal documents." It was yet another disappointment. Even in death Ahmed was making my life difficult. Noticing my frustration, the police chief advised me to file an appeal with the state prosecutor for a "confirmation of death." If Ahmed's body was not formally identified within a few months, the appeal would allow me to take the necessary steps to have his death officially registered based on witness accounts. It's common practice now because so many terrorists are killed in remote areas and are buried out there by their friends. The police chief seemed just as relieved as I was. He confided to a friend of mine who'd gone to the station with me: "Her husband caused a lot of problems. For us, his family, and the whole village. He was a real idiot. Things were just fine when he was with his friends and family. Then he started acting like a jerk, and what did it get him? His wife is a widow now, and his child is fatherless. And he ended up slaughtered like a dog." Alone in my bed that night, I cried. Tears of relief. Tears of exhaustion, joy, and who knows what else? Tears of sadness, for sure. Even though I was happy to escape the nightmare I'd been living, I wish my married life hadn't ended the way it did. I wish my son's father, a man I lived with for three short months and loved passionately, hadn't wound up as nothing more than a headless body at the bottom of a ravine on the Mitidja Plain.

And so I returned to Hai Bounab after not having set foot there in more than a year and a half. It was spring, and the land was spectacularly beautiful, as it always is then. It's hard to resist the urge to roll on the green carpet of grass dotted with yellow daisies. That's what I used to do as a carefree young girl. The foliage in the orchards was as dense as ever when I arrived. Here and there, a few oranges that the farmers had overlooked were clinging to the branches. Exactly as it used to be. This region has always brought prosperity to anyone who knows how to cultivate it properly. The French colonists were the first. When you look at such an idyllic scene, it's hard to understand how the people who live here could possibly be inclined to violence.

I ran into Ali in Eucalyptus Village's main square, just a few yards from police headquarters. He was wearing a communal guard uniform.[4] I didn't recognize him at first. He is just forty-five but already looks like an old man. It's hardly been two years, yet he has aged considerably. His features are drawn, and deep furrows etch his face. The day I ran into him, he was helping the police patrol the roadblock and was carrying a rifle on his shoulder. I stopped to say hello. When he comes face to face with me, he still has trouble concealing his feelings of guilt. He couldn't avoid bringing up the topic: "Can you believe it? After all I did for them, they wanted to take my daughters from me and force me to build a hideout for them under my house." I didn't say anything. The discussion would have been pointless and all too painful. And besides, I had other problems. I just asked how his daughters were doing. They were friends of mine. I don't hold anything against him. Ever since he turned my husband and his friends in, Ali has been living in an abandoned hammam in Eucalyptus, where the police arranged for him to stay with his wife and children. They were afraid the terrorists might seek revenge. He's not the only one who was forced to move or run away. Terrorism has caused so many people to flee, torn apart scores of families.

Ali had been one of the GIA's most trusted allies. Seeing him at his new job made me realize how much things have changed. Life is back to normal, except that the joy that existed before is gone—that special joy unique to country people. It's as if a leaden cloud is looming over the region. How could it be otherwise when every man you meet from the moment you approach the area is armed? As soon as I was in Hai Bounab—about a mile and a half away—I went to visit my mother. She had moved back into our old house barely two weeks earlier. She hadn't returned to the village—nor had I—since the day our former neighbors pointed their newly acquired guns at us. We were so happy to be going back home that we'd forgotten that in their eyes we were first and foremost a family of terrorists. They used to be our friends, but that day they threatened to set fire to the truck carrying our furniture and belongings. We promptly turned around and drove off. It was thanks to the police that our house wasn't destroyed. They let a needy family stay there but made it clear to them that the arrangement wasn't permanent. They would only be looking after the premises temporarily. On the way to my mother's, I had to walk by my own house. It's been gutted by fire and partially demolished. Even so, there's a family squatting there. My mother tells me they're decent people. Their house was razed by an explosion. They said they'd vacate whenever I wanted.

Everyone in our village believed that the GIA had taken over. Either that or they pretended to. I had no choice. I had to believe it was true because I was the wife of Ahmed Chaabani, the emir of Hai Bounab and the surrounding area. I know for a fact that by remaining silent and providing logistical support we were all responsible for letting terrorism take root and grow here. The terrorists had complete control for more than three years. The community condoned their actions, accepted everything they did, and didn't revolt against the GIA until it started terrorizing the very people who had aided and abetted the group. The turnaround was just as sudden as it was violent. But I simply accepted things the way they were. I loved my husband, and that's all there was to it. I forgave him everything. And I've paid dearly for it.

2

My mother and father are first cousins. They spent their childhood in Douera, a farming community about twelve miles west
of Algiers. Their parents betrothed them to each other when
they were just children. In rural areas, girls are often promised
to a cousin or a neighbor's son at birth. My parents grew up
knowing they'd be together for the rest of their lives. It was a
good match: they realized at a very young age that they were in
love. That's why they were so impatient to wed. They couldn't
wait. My mother was barely fourteen. My father was seventeen.
I was born a year later. There has always been a strong bond
between my mother and me because of the small age difference
between us. In fact, people who don't know us automatically
assume we're friends.

Ours was a poor peasant family, but the atmosphere at home
was always warm and loving. The love my mother and father
share—even to this day—has helped us overcome the obstacles
that came our way. Despite the hardships, we weren't destitute.
There was always enough food on the table—and it was good
fresh food, too. My father was a farmhand at the time, so we
had fruit and vegetables in the house year round. He managed to get eggs, milk, and occasionally meat and honey from
the neighboring farmers. They all bartered among themselves.
There were a number of farms in the area. They stretched over
hundreds of acres and produced a variety of crops and livestock.
The agricultural revolution was at its peak. [1]

My father is a very nice man, but he's definitely strange. He
likes to kid around—a lot less these days though. All he's ever
wanted to do is relax and have fun. Nothing else matters to

him. People out in the country may be quite conservative and traditional, but they know how to have a good time—in their own way. My father was so in love with my mother that he was wildly jealous. About two years after they were married, a man told him he'd had an affair with my mother when she was still single. My father couldn't understand how my mother, who'd been engaged to him since birth, could have cheated on him like that. Without bothering to find out if it was true, he sent her back to her parents and kept me at home with him. My grandmother was living with us, so she took care of me. But once my mother was gone, my father got very depressed. He started drinking and took it out on me when he'd had one too many. He'd beat me and then start crying after he realized what he'd done. He came up with the perfect excuse to visit my mother and used it whenever he couldn't stand being away from her any longer: he said she ought to be able to see her daughter. So he'd take me to her parents' house where she was staying and use the visit as a pretext to spend time with her himself. As it happened, she got pregnant after one of those visits. When my grandfather found out, he forced his son-in-law to take his wife back. But my father was ashamed and refused to admit he was the one who got her pregnant. The case went to court and it was only after a judge intervened that my father gave in. The truth of the matter was that my father worried that the neighbors would start gossiping once they saw my mother pregnant after having been separated from her husband for so long. Yet, at the same time, he was so happy she was coming home that he invited the whole village to celebrate the event. No one in the family had a clue as to what was going on in his mind.

When I was six, the local authorities gave us a house in another farming village on the outskirts of Cheraga, about nine miles west of Algiers. It was a beautiful place with several rooms, a kitchen, an inner courtyard, and tiled floors. My father was a farmhand at a neighboring estate.[2] It was wonderful there.

They enrolled me in the village school. I got top grades, and my teachers liked me. I have fond memories of that period of my life. We were a happy family with no problems to speak of. It lasted nine years, but unfortunately my father's irresponsibility brought an end to our bliss.

My father is a loafer—with a taste for luxury to boot. One day he decided to quit his job at the estate. The thought of having no income terrified my mother. My father told her he wasn't getting along with his coworkers, but the real story was a little different. His coworkers didn't appreciate the fact that he was always slacking off while they slaved away from morning till night. They complained that after two or three days' work, he'd stop, claiming the soil was no good and nothing would grow on it. He was constantly griping. Actually, it was because of him and another worker that the farm's yield was so poor. Proof that the land was fertile came later when the estate was reorganized and management was turned over to a group of farmworkers.[3] It produced all sorts of fruit and vegetables, even exotic fruit we'd never seen before. The people who worked the farm got rich. Now my father regrets what he did. But back then, he had only one goal in mind: he wanted to own a car. And to make his dream come true, he decided to sell the house.

That's how we lost our home in Cheraga, the house we loved so much and where we were so happy. My mother insists to this day that when we lost that place our luck went with it. My father sold the property for 630,000 dinars and used the money to buy another one in Hai Bounab—a tiny village in the Eucalyptus district near Baraki, about twelve miles east of Algiers.[4] That house was totally different from the one we had before. It was smaller and not nearly as comfortable. There was no electricity or running water. The floor was nothing but a slab of cold concrete. It took my mother a long time to get used to the new house. My brothers and sisters didn't like it either. I cried and cried, and didn't speak to my father for days. That's when I dropped out of school. I was in the ninth grade and the new school just wasn't right for me. It was too far away. It was in Eucalyptus, which was almost an hour's walk through the fields. Getting there in winter was a real ordeal. When it rained, I was soaked and covered in mud up to my knees by the time I made it to class. The only thing I could think about was going home to change and get warm. Besides, I was fifteen and all my friends were in Cheraga. On top of it all, I didn't think my new teachers were very friendly, so I decided I'd rather stay home. It was a way of getting even with my father. I knew if I dropped out it would really upset him. Since he couldn't read or write he had high hopes for my future. A lot of farmworkers back then counted on their children's education to get them out of poverty. My mother was a bit disappointed, too, but it was a blessing in disguise for her because she had someone to help out around the house. She had trouble looking after the whole family all by herself. I was the oldest of seven children. After me came my two brothers. Boys aren't expected to do housework. And so a new life began for me. Each morning I went to draw water from the village well, about two hundred yards from the house. I did the laundry, washed the dishes, and so on. My mother concentrated her energy on cooking and taking care of the youngest children.

Buying that house was a disaster for all of us—except my father. It was a deal for him. He paid only 240,000 dinars for it. He had enough left over to buy the car he'd always dreamed of for 309,000 dinars and still put some money aside. Naturally, everyone thought he was being foolish, but he tried to justify buying the car by arguing that he could use it as a taxi and make more money than on the farm. He didn't admit it, but his real intention was to live off the leftover cash and not have to work. And that's what he started doing. Unfortunately, the car he bought was in pretty bad shape. It was used, and the man who sold it to him was a swindler. After a few months, my father sold it at a loss, then bought another that turned out to be just as unreliable. He kept doing that until he'd gone through all his savings. During those two years, my father spent most of his time sleeping. Since he never woke up before mid-afternoon, he wasn't tired at night and did everything he could to get us to stay up and keep him company. Sometimes, when he was bored, he'd have us fix him something to eat at the most ridiculous hours. But he was so nice to us that we always gave in to his whims. It wasn't until he was completely broke that he realized he needed to go back to work. This was after one of our neighbors lectured him: "You've got lots of kids. What makes you think you can just sleep all day long?" Out of embarrassment, my father accepted a street-cleaning job the neighbor had found for him. (That neighbor was killed two years later by members of the GIA because he refused to collaborate with them.) My father showed little enthusiasm for his new occupation. The town authorities constantly complained about him, claiming he did sloppy work.

One thing he never got tired of doing, though, was having children. Three more were born after we moved to Hai Bounab. My mother, who is now thirty-seven and a grandmother, is pregnant for the eleventh time. She's due in two months.

My father worked as a street sweeper in Eucalyptus for nearly two years. He was fired when they found out his son-in-law was the leader of a GIA cell.

3

Little by little, we grew accustomed to our new life in Hai Bounab. As time went by, the house took on a different feeling. Despite our limited resources, my mother and I furnished it and managed to make it comfortable and inviting. Thanks to the warm, friendly support of our neighbors, our initial disappointment faded and we were able to create an environment similar to the one in Cheraga. Over time, Hai Bounab had totally changed. It no longer resembled the desolate rural community that it had been when we arrived. Facilities sprang up that hadn't existed before: a school, a health center, little stores, and the like. When we first got there, the tiny village was just being built. It was practically nothing but walls, and we were cut off from everything. Then we got electricity, which gave us access to television. Satellite dishes soon appeared all over the village. We used to watch French stations and broadcasts from other Arab countries, but never when my father was around because some of the scenes in the movies they showed were too sexually explicit. Later, two grocery stores opened and everyone was ecstatic. We could finally buy basic necessities without having to walk an hour through the fields. That made our lives much easier.

Hai Bounab is comprised of three small clusters of houses. There are about a hundred homes in all, but each lodges two or three brothers and their wives, children, grandparents, and sometimes aunts and cousins. Consequently, the population is fairly dense.

The neighbors were a tremendous help to us in the beginning. Since my father was unemployed most of the time, workers from the nearby farming enterprise always sent us our share of fruit and vegetables when they picked up their own. Everyone got along well—even with us, the only outsiders. All the other families belonged to the same tribe, the Souaghi tribe from Ouled Soltane in the Medea region. Looking back, I can truly say we were like one big family. Whatever happened to one of us affected us all.

The happiest day for the villagers came when the grade school opened. That was in 1992, a year after we moved to Hai Bounab. They took up a collection to celebrate the occasion and prepared a delicious lamb couscous with nice fresh vegetables and a salad. We had an abundance of fruit from the orchards. The women made cakes, tea, and coffee. All the construction workers who'd helped build the school were invited. We'd been promising them a feast ever since the day they laid the first stone, and they wouldn't have missed it for the world. Employees from the Eucalyptus town hall were there, too. Even the police got to share in the festivities. We sent lunchboxes overflowing with food to the ones on duty who couldn't come. The meal was served in the schoolyard for good luck. Celebrating the completion of a new building with good food brings prosperity, according to the old women in the village. After the meal was over and the men had left, the old women went through each classroom with small incense burners to ward off the devil and the evil eye, as they did for every new building. The people of Hai Bounab were happy for their sons, but even happier for their daughters. Now they wouldn't have to worry about them crossing the fields morning and evening and getting home after dark in winter.

Everybody in Hai Bounab is more or less religious in a natural and spontaneous way. Before the GIA came, we practiced our faith as tradition required but no more than that and, admittedly, not very strictly. No one worried about the next person as far as religion was concerned. We didn't even have a mosque in our village. The few who wanted to attend public prayers on

Fridays went all the way to Eucalyptus—mostly older people, because it gave them a chance to see friends there. Religion was like politics: hardly any villagers got involved. They had too much work to do in the fields to take time out for that. Some of our neighbors did belong to the Islamic Salvation Front before it was disbanded, but even the party leaders contained their activities to the district's administrative center. They never came to Hai Bounab.

I was the life of the village. Our neighbors were especially fond of me because I was always willing to pitch in and help the women with their chores. Whenever one of them had a baby (a frequent occurrence), I was the first to show up to take care of the other children and tend to the housework. They knew they could count on me anytime. I was even more popular with the girls my age. I initiated new ways of doing things in the village, like going to get water from the well. Before, only the boys got to do that. I had fewer inhibitions than the other girls. They'd spent their lives in the country. I was more of a city girl because I'd lived in Cheraga, so I wasn't as shy. It quickly became a pleasure instead of a chore to fetch water, a time to relax and have fun. When it was really hot, we'd go for a dip. We used to jump in with our clothes on. I was always the first, of course. It took a while for the other girls to follow my example. Some of them thought I was too bold, but once they got over their bashfulness, they took a liking to it and had a great time. The boys would watch us from a distance. Sometimes they'd see to it that their paths crossed ours, and we'd chat with them for a while—not too long, though. We didn't want our parents to see. Once in a while the boys would whistle at us from far away or sing songs and send us little notes. We used to pick the fruit the workers had left on the trees at the end of the season. There were oranges, mandarins, peaches, apricots, and almonds. We'd eat some on the way back, but there was so much that we all had enough left over to take home.

I showed the other girls how to crochet, embroider, and weave rugs out of remnants of cloth — things I learned from my aunts in Cheraga. After the housework was done, we would go out on the porch of one of the houses, spread out a mat, and spend the afternoon there together. I'll never forget the evenings during Ramadan. We'd stay out until the men came back from the café and the women returned from visiting the neighbors. We sang and danced and tasted the different cakes we'd each made at home. It was a month of pure delight. We really looked forward to it. On the night of the Mulud, we'd stay out till dawn.[1] My father never said anything, nor did the other fathers. It was normal. We were happy, and any occasion to celebrate was good. Those girls were my friends. They knew about my relationship with Ahmed. There was Saloua, Hakima, Djamila, Rachida, and Fatiha.

Saloua and Fatiha were later decapitated.

4

Before moving to Hai Bounab, Ahmed had lived with his mother and brothers in Benramdane—a remote village in the Mitidja region. But his family came from Kef Lakhdar in the Saharan Atlas Mountains overlooking the city of Medea. That's where he grew up. He said his mother and father married for love. Like mine. But his father had a weakness for women, especially married ones. He had a terrible reputation in Benramdane, and his brothers disliked him because of it. They told him he was the rotten apple of the family. He had affairs with women from other villages, and one day, the husband of one of the women he was involved with decided to kill him. The man happened to be his friend, so he invited him over for dinner and put poison in his food. Ahmed's father died a few days later in intense pain. His brothers had seen him bent over and writhing but thought it was just stomach cramps. Little did they suspect he'd been poisoned. After several days, they became concerned and rushed him to the hospital when he starting losing his hair for no apparent reason. The doctor determined it was poisoning and told them it was too late to save him. The brothers were quick to figure out who the culprit was, but no one pressed charges against him. The family was so embarrassed that they just wanted to cover up the whole incident. Ahmed's mother was two months pregnant with her fourth son at the time. He's the same age as me. We were born on the same day. Ahmed was the third son. Her brothers-in-law didn't like her. On the day of her husband's funeral, they kicked her out of the house but kept the children.

The three boys had a hard time coping with their mother's

absence, coinciding as it did with their father's death. They felt everyone had abandoned them, especially since their uncles and uncles' wives treated them like slaves. They didn't show the boys the slightest bit of affection. Although they were just children, their sole function was to work. The oldest was barely eight, and Ahmed three. Because he was the youngest, Ahmed was the most restless. Consequently, he got a beating every day. Despite his young age, they sent him out into the fields with his brothers to tend the cows and sheep. They'd be out there the whole day with nothing to eat. When they got home in the evening, they had to make do with leftovers—if there were any. Their cousins went to school, but the three brothers were never enrolled, even though they were living under the same roof. Their uncles claimed they couldn't send all the boys in the family to school because some of them had to take care of the livestock. Regardless, Ahmed did learn the Arabic alphabet by attending the Koranic school for a few months. That's what enabled him to read and write when he was older. He was very unhappy living with his uncles and ran away several times. More than once he tried to see his mother, who had returned to Benramdane and was staying with her brothers, but they didn't want to have anything to do with their nephews either. Every time Ahmed appeared, they sent for his paternal grandfather to come get him—which he did, typically beating the boy repeatedly with a stick. On one occasion Ahmed hid in the woods for two days. Shivering and racked with hunger, he finally came out, thinking his grandfather had left. But the man was still there waiting for him. Ahmed had no alternative but to follow him home in tears.

Ahmed was clever and full of energy. From the time he was little, he loved money and was always finding ways to get it. When he was just a child, he told the farmers in the area he'd tend their sheep and cows for a small fee while he was looking after his uncles' livestock. He and his brothers had a plan: they would save as much money as possible—enough to allow them to join their mother so they could all live together far from their uncles' house. By age fifteen Ahmed felt he was big enough to make another attempt. Although he was the youngest, he was the one who prompted his brothers to follow him, and one day the three of them showed up at their mother's. Realizing that now they were dealing with young adults, not children, their maternal uncles didn't dare try to send them back—especially when they saw that the boys hadn't come empty-handed. They had enough money to get by for a while. One of the uncles emptied out a chicken coop for them to stay in temporarily.

The Chaabanis (that's their last name) were what you could call a hardworking family. Having her four sons there with her gave Ahmed's mother strength. She had been pregnant with the youngest when her husband died, and now the boy was an adolescent. She pitched in, too, making sweets that her sons sold at the market in Benramdane. And she raised hens and sold the eggs to the villagers. The boys got jobs as porters at the wholesale market in Bougara.[1] They were strong, and the vendors liked their stamina for hard work. By scrimping and saving, the Chaabanis were able to amass a bit of money. But it still wasn't enough to buy or rent a house and move out of the chicken coop where they were living. Then one day luck smiled on Ahmed. He found a wallet in the street with thirty thousand dinars in it. The local gossips claimed he had stolen the money, but he swore by all the saints in heaven that he really did find it. That money, together with what the family had saved from doing odd jobs, made it possible for them to buy a house in Hai Bounab, right near ours, for 150,000 dinars. True, at that price all they could get was a shell. It was nothing more than cement walls with crude openings instead of doors and windows, but it was spacious and had several rooms. A lot of people buy houses in that condition: first because the housing shortage is so bad and the most important thing is to have a roof over your head. And second because houses like that are obviously much less expensive than ones that are completely finished. Buyers can fix them up the way they want.

Ahmed's mother continued her business activities in Hai Bounab. She knew how to do so many things. In addition to selling eggs and sweets, she made and sold rugs. The Chaabanis did well enough to buy a van, and the oldest brother used it to set up a transportation service between Hai Bounab and Baraki. After that, they converted a room in their house that looked onto the street into a grocery store. The second brother managed it. Then they bought two cows, and their mother started selling milk, whey, and butter. Dairy products made from cow's milk according to traditional methods are highly prized by city dwellers and very expensive. Everyone in the family worked, but it was Ahmed's mother who kept all the money. Yet whenever the family purchased anything of value, they'd put it in the oldest son's name. That's the custom here. And so, little by little, they became one of the most well-to-do families in the village. They completed the construction work on their house and furnished it fairly comfortably. In short, they had everything they needed. The oldest brother, Bilal, was very devout, but he was also extremely self-centered. He was never satisfied and always wanted more for himself. He wouldn't share anything with his brothers. And because he was his mother's favorite, she backed him in everything he did. He wasn't mean like Nouredine, the younger brother, though. Later, Nouredine caused me a lot of grief.

One day, the "patriots" decapitated both Bilal and Nouredine and threw their bodies into a ravine.[2]

5

And so it was there, in Hai Bounab, in the spring of 1992, that the man who was to become my husband — and virtually at the same time an emir in the GIA — came to live with his family. Their house was very close to ours. The street number of my parents' house is "1" and the Chaabanis' is "2." Ahmed was eighteen back then and more like an adult than an adolescent. The suffering he'd endured as a child had hardened him. I was sixteen. Now that I think about it, he was a real thug. But he had so much charm that he could get almost anybody to like him. His behavior was unusual for our quiet little village. For example, he courted all the girls in the neighborhood and made no attempt to hide it. The parents were shocked, to say the least. They were very conservative and felt the way he was acting was a breach of the most basic rules of etiquette. But his worst vice was theft. He used to steal fruit from the orchards nearby and sell it at the market. There was no holding him back. He did the most reprehensible things. Everybody kept an eye on him — fathers worried about their daughters, and farmers worried about their crops. In addition, he succeeded in dragging my younger brother into his schemes. He's the one who got us into the bad habit of stealing. None of us used to do that before.

The Chaabanis were the envy of everyone because all the children were boys. Having several males in the family is a sign of future prosperity. And since fetching water had become girls' work, my mother told me I should go offer Madame Chaabani my services. That was the custom: the neighbors helped each other out so that no one would be in need of anything. When I knocked at their door, Ahmed answered. I think I was attracted to him from that moment but wasn't really aware of it. It was the first time I had ever had such a sensation. It was strange yet pleasant. But I automatically shut it out. Where I come from, it's frowned upon for girls to think about boys that way. The fear of dishonor had been instilled in me at an early age. Taboos were not to be broken. I think Ahmed took a liking to me, too, because he started teasing me even though we'd just met. I have to admit I sort of liked it. Anyway, he made me laugh. But I told myself I shouldn't let him get away with acting like that with me because if the neighbors ever found out, they'd think I had no morals. So to save face and prevent the gossip from starting, I told his brother, Bilal, about it. He gave Ahmed a good talking-to. As the oldest in the family, Bilal was responsible for the household. He insisted on maintaining good relations with the neighbors and didn't want the family's arrival in Hai Bounab to start off with an argument, especially one of that nature, which is precisely what would have happened if I'd mentioned it to my father. But I didn't because, deep down, I didn't want to spoil my chances of seeing Ahmed again. In fact, while his brother was scolding him, I laughed impetuously on purpose. To excite him. I'll always look back with nostalgia and joy on the first time we met. Little did I know then where it would all lead.

From that day on, I couldn't stop thinking about him. Two months after the Chaabanis moved to Hai Bounab, another family came to live near us. They had a daughter, Naima, who was a year older than me. She was nice and very pretty. We soon became friends. In all innocence, I confided in her about my feelings for Ahmed, thinking she'd help get him interested in me. Instead, I found them together one day. She was at the window, he was outside, and they were talking, with their arms around each other. It was my first heartbreak, and I told Naima so, but she didn't care. I was devastated and couldn't stop crying. Luckily for me, Naima was just as flighty as Ahmed. Before moving to Hai Bounab, she had had another boyfriend who lived in

Eucalyptus, and she was still going with him. He went to the same school as she did, in Baraki. Naima was not as discreet as the other girls in our village and let herself be seen wherever she went with him — to Chrea, the movies in Algiers, the beach, and so on. Ahmed eventually found out and promptly dropped her. The turn of events obviously worked in my favor. I was finally going to be able to get back the man I loved. The incident made me understand my true feelings for him and spurred me on to start things moving more quickly. I decided to let him know exactly how I felt before some other girl came into the picture, and I found an easy way to do it: I got his attention as he was walking by my house one day and stared at him with a suggestive smile. He understood what I meant and didn't waste any time. He wrote me a note and had my little sister deliver it. He said he was very attracted to me and wanted to get more serious. I answered just as quickly, telling him I wanted that, too, so long as my father, brothers, and neighbors knew nothing about it. There was just one detail that had to be worked out: how could I see him without arousing suspicion? Knowing my parents would be going away in two days, I arranged to meet him as soon as they left. He started talking about marriage right away and went to ask my father for my hand the next day. While my father thoroughly appreciated Ahmed's hardworking side, he didn't take him the least bit seriously. What he really disliked about Ahmed was his underlying vice: stealing. I felt the same way and said so to Ahmed. I even tried to make our relationship contingent on it. "If you love me, quit stealing," I told him. But there was no way to stop him. Realizing he'd never change, I tried to rationalize his behavior by telling myself it was normal for him to act like a thug because he'd been raised without a family, left on his own, and deprived of affection. My father turned down Ahmed's marriage proposal without even taking the time to ponder it or talk to me about it.

But that didn't stop us from seeing each other. We found ways to meet in isolated spots in Hai Bounab or rode over to Baraki whenever we could. Not too far. My girlfriends were in on it and so were my little sisters—but not my brothers. Whenever any of my sisters saw him go by, they'd immediately come tell me and let me know where he was. If it was close by, I'd run to join him for a while. We always met in secret. But that was fine. We were happy the way things were.

We had a neighbor who watched everything everybody did. She was a real busybody. What's more, she was extremely jealous. Envious. One day she caught me with Ahmed and told my mother about it. My mother had had no idea I was seeing him. She blew up at me. "So now you're hanging around with boys," she yelled. "And with that crook on top of it. Do you want to disgrace your family?" She even hit me. From that day on, she made me do all the heavy chores around the house—chores I didn't have to do before. "If you're old enough to be dating, you're old enough to work," she said time and again. The worst part of it was that since she wouldn't let me go out, I couldn't see Ahmed. I felt the treatment was unfair and managed to win her over by telling her the whole story. But she couldn't understand why, of all the boys in the village, I chose the one she considered to be the least respectable: the one who stole the neighbors' fruit to buy himself Reeboks and new jeans, the compulsive cruiser, the one who always got into fights and usually had a black eye. Nevertheless, when she saw that her preaching was having no effect on me, she finally accepted the fact that I was truly in love with him. There was nothing she could do about it, so she admitted defeat. Actually, she and I have always been accomplices, more or less: "You can go on seeing him, but just be careful about your reputation." It seems she had noticed the recent change in my behavior. When Ahmed didn't come by to see me, I was like a madwoman, crying for no apparent reason and doing crazy things. One day I was so upset that he hadn't contacted me in over a week that I picked up a pair of scissors without even realizing it and started whacking off my hair.

Ahmed was gone much of the time. He claimed his work carting things around at the wholesale market wasn't paying the way it used to. He wanted to make a lot of money. And fast. He had a strong business sense. Together with some of his friends, he started organizing trips to places far from Hai Bounab, even as far as Setif, to buy smuggled goods and resell them in Algiers.[1] From there, he'd bring back dishes, clothes, food, and so on—all imported. He'd go to Libya, too, even though he didn't have a passport. All he had was his national identity card and a driver's license. He crossed the southern border and took long, roundabout routes to get where he was going. He'd bring back the same kinds of things from Libya, along with jewelry, cosmetics, and sometimes cars, which he sold intact or piece by piece for parts.

Later, he would be dealing in weapons and explosives.

6

My relationship with Ahmed continued without incident. He had built up a lucrative business, but I never asked him for anything. I didn't want him to think I was materialistic, like the other girls. And he never thought of giving me anything. He wasn't the considerate type. The only gift he gave me before we were married was a copper ring, as a sign of loyalty. He told me not to wear any other jewelry. Even though it was just copper, I was thrilled, and cherished it as if it were the most beautiful of gifts. He sent me letters, too, with poems he'd written and things he didn't have time to say when we were together. And he gave me cassettes. His favorite singer was Cheb Hasni.[1] He was his idol. Every time we saw each other, Ahmed would sing Hasni's songs to me. He had a beautiful voice. His favorite was *Tal ghiabek ya ghazali*.[2]

Ahmed was very headstrong. When he decided to do something, he never thought about the consequences. One evening, for example, he knocked at the window of the bedroom I shared with my sisters. It looked onto the street. He knew my father was working that night (before becoming a street sweeper, he was a night watchman in a factory for a few months). Ahmed wanted to take advantage of my father's absence to be with me. He also knew I slept by the window. He knocked, but I didn't wake up, so he broke the shutters. It was summer and the windows were open. He poked a long steel wire into the room and used it to try to wake me. He couldn't climb into the bedroom because of the security bars on the windows. I've always been a sound sleeper, so when he finally managed to wake me, I was dazed and wondering what was going on. As soon as I figured it out, I went into a rage and let him know his stupidity could get me in a lot of trouble. All he said was that he had no recollection of coming to my house, that he had walked over like some kind of robot. From then on, he showed up every night—with my consent. Then one day his brother, Nouredine, caught him. But I was the one Nouredine balled out. He called me a slut and accused me of setting a trap for Ahmed. When he saw how afraid I was that my parents might find out about Ahmed's nightly visits, he seized the opportunity to try to seduce me and tried to blackmail me. When I snubbed him, he threatened to get even one day. I realized how impulsive Ahmed could be and decided it was better not to tell him about Nouredine's offensive behavior. I was afraid the two of them might get into a fight over me. Even so, Ahmed noticed I wasn't quite the same after that. I was scared Nouredine would tell my brothers about it. They were younger, but they still had authority over me.

A few days after that incident, Nouredine got me into another predicament. This one turned my life upside down. I'd sent Ahmed a letter, and he forgot to take it out of his pants pocket. Nouredine found it. It was the chance he'd been waiting for to get even with me. He promptly showed the letter to his mother, who in turn caused a big uproar. Standing at her front door, she yelled out to my parents: "Hold back your girls! I know you'd do anything to get one of my sons. And I've got the proof now!" I was the only one to blame as far as everyone was concerned. When my father questioned me, I denied everything. My mother took my side, but the news spread through the village like wildfire. Our family had been disgraced. My father forbade me to leave the house from that day on, and I wasn't able to talk to Ahmed for almost six months. He disappeared for three of those months, hiding at his uncles' house in Benramdane. Then he showed up one day as if nothing had happened. As soon as he got back, he had one of the little neighbor girls bring me a message saying he was sorry about what had happened and claiming it wasn't his fault. But I didn't answer him. Not that time or any of the others.

One night when I was in bed and just starting to doze off, he knocked at my window, as he'd done before. I thought it was probably him but pretended not to hear. As chance would have it, my brother went outside at that very moment. Afraid my brother might see him, Ahmed jumped over the wall into our yard. My mother hadn't gone to sleep yet. She heard the noise, went running into the yard, and saw him. As if that wasn't bad enough, when he jumped, he landed on a tub full of dirty dishes. The clattering was so loud it woke up the whole household. This time my mother couldn't cover for me. My brothers were furious. They decided to tell my father every-thing. When he got home from work the next morning, my mother explained it all to him before my brothers had a chance, but she managed to convey some of their venom. My father felt humiliated. Ahmed had been disrespectful to him. "If this continues, that boy and our daughter are going to drown us in shame. We have to get her away from here," he announced. A few hours later, without saying a word or scolding me, he took me to my uncles' in Cheraga. I felt really sorry for my father that day. I was uncomfortable in his presence. I would have preferred it if he'd yelled at me or even hit me. Anything would have been better than that heavy silence he had locked himself in. Of all his children I was his favorite, and I had disappointed him.

I remained shut away in Cheraga for two years. My uncles watched my every move. I'd become a disgrace to the family. I didn't see Ahmed in those two years, but I did get news about him every so often. Then, one day, my father came to tell me Ahmed had officially asked to marry me. He'd tried twice be-fore, but my father refused each time. In the interim, however, Ahmed had joined the GIA and was terrorizing the village. My father was still fiercely opposed to the marriage and said so to Ahmed but not in very strong terms. Like everyone else, my father was afraid of the GIA. When he came by to give me the news, he shared his apprehensions with my aunt—but not with me, because where we live a father doesn't talk about such things with his daughter. "If I don't say yes, I know he can take her against my will," he told my aunt. So rather than suffer the affront of seeing his daughter taken by force, he preferred bending to Ahmed's wishes. My aunt went to pieces. She hated terrorism and terrorists more than anything, but she had to face the facts: not even the most foolhardy of us would have dared stand up to the GIA. Personally, I have to admit that the two years Ahmed and I were apart hadn't changed my feelings toward him in the least. I was thrilled to see him again. I wasn't thinking about what went along with it. Besides, I didn't entirely believe what they said about him. People, my brothers included, had told me on more than one occasion that Ahmed and his friends had become terrorists. But I was sure it was all just lies to get me to break up with him. It was Saturday. "If you agree to it," my father said, "be ready on Wednesday. I'll be back to pick you up."

I started getting my things together. I was ecstatic.

7

I looked out the window of the car taking me back to my parents' in Hai Bounab and spotted Ahmed with some of his friends. They were building the house we were going to live in. In this part of the country, most construction work is pretty helter-skelter. You don't have to own land or have a permit to build. You just put up a few cinder block walls anywhere you want and call it home. Ours was tiny and unfinished, but seeing it filled me with happiness. We were married three days later at the town hall in El Harrach. The traditional ceremony was to take place two days later. Once we completed the formalities with the mayor and returned to our respective homes, Ahmed came to see my parents. He insisted on talking to me in private, despite my father's disapproval. So long as the marriage hadn't been consummated, my father still considered me under his guardianship. But my father's objections didn't dissuade Ahmed, and my father finally gave in to his request. Ahmed wanted to tell me about the changes he'd undergone and probably about his new life as a member of the GIA. But he didn't have time to do that because he was so taken aback by the changes he saw in me. One of my cousins who had gotten me ready for the wedding had colored and styled my hair. She'd plucked my eyebrows and put makeup on me, too. When Ahmed came in and saw me like that, he let out a scream. Then he started reciting incantations and calling on God. His reaction took me totally by surprise. Before our separation, he often told me he liked natural-looking women, but I never thought a little makeup would get him so worked up. "Why did you do that to yourself?" he asked. Not knowing how to respond, I told him: "I didn't do it. It was the hairdresser. Besides, all brides like to look their prettiest on their wedding day." Apparently he didn't share that opinion. His voice took on a solemn tone as he announced: "From now on, you won't be going to the hammam anymore, or the hairdresser's. And this is the last time I want to see you wearing makeup." I was stunned. I let him know how astounded I was that he would make the hammam off limits. "Baths are sinful," he said. "Women shouldn't go naked, even in front of other women." Then he added: "Put on your *khimar*.[1] And don't let me ever see that coloring in your hair again." That was when I began to wonder if what they'd told me about him might in fact have some grain of truth to it. To find out for sure, I decided to push him a little further: "Sing me one of Cheb Hasni's songs, like you used to. You know, I cried a lot the day he was assassinated." His answer left no room for discussion: "I forbid you to cry over that *taghout*.[2] He deserved to die. He was using his songs to lead young people away from the path of righteousness." The message was loud and clear, but I persisted, reminding him of when he used to go around with his radio glued to his ear listening to his idol, Cheb Hasni, and how he knew every single one of his songs by heart. He fired back in an even harsher tone: "That was when I was living in the age of ignorance."[3]

There was no longer any doubt. What I'd been told about him was true. After our two-year separation, he was an entirely different man from the one I'd known before. There's no way I can describe my disappointment. It wasn't at all what I had imagined getting back together would be like. A knot of anxiety tightened around my heart. It was so strong that, as soon as Ahmed was out of the room, I started screaming to keep from suffocating. My mother came running in to ask what was wrong. When I told her what I'd learned, she only had one thing to say to me: "We warned you. You're the one who wanted this. Now you'll have to live with your decision." I realized I had just made a huge mistake. But strangely, and despite all proof to the contrary, I clung to one tiny thread of hope: maybe it was all just a big act. Or maybe I'd be able to change him once we were married. Yet, in all sincerity, what counted most for me at that moment was being his wife and living with him. I don't believe I would have left him, no matter what happened that day.

The cinder block rooms Ahmed had built for us still weren't finished. The day before the traditional wedding ceremony, he borrowed some corrugated sheet metal my father had on hand so he could put a roof over the structure. The lack of comfort didn't bother me in the least. Ahmed gave me thirty-five thousand dinars for my dowry. I used the money to buy two outfits and two gold chains. My mother was the one who decided what to get—a bride doesn't enter her husband's house without jewelry. The purchases weren't exorbitant, but there was nothing left over to cover the cost of the wedding preparations. Since my father had voiced his opposition to the marriage in no uncertain terms, he refused to lift a finger to help us save face. True, he couldn't afford to be extravagant on a street sweeper's salary, but he could have borrowed a little money from his brothers. My mother stepped in to take care of the arrangements and make sure the festivities went on as expected. Once again the neighbors came to my rescue. Some of them brought cakes, others meat for the meal.

On the day of the wedding, Ahmed and his brothers were supposed to come get me at around 11 o'clock in the morning. I waited until 2 o'clock. His brothers never showed up. Their mother wouldn't let them. She was opposed to the marriage, too. As for Ahmed, he arrived with his friends in three brand-new cars—two Mercedes Phantoms and a third car. I'm not sure of the make, but it was just as expensive. When I asked why he was so late, he said he'd been with the "group."[4] His response was proof the "group" was so important to him that it even took precedence over his own wedding.

His mother made her hostility known to me from day one. She'd been resentful ever since the last incident, when she swore she'd never have anything to do with me or my family. So, like her sons, she didn't come to my parents' house to escort me to hers as tradition dictates. She had the wife of her oldest son do it. But I didn't make a fuss about it and made up my mind that things would get better over time.

When I went into the bedroom, I noticed some cassettes on the nightstand. I was overjoyed. For a few moments, I thought Ahmed still listened to music, the way he used to. So he hadn't changed as much as it seemed. I ran over to the cassette player to listen to one of the tapes. It was verses from the Koran. What a letdown. My aunts who had come with me felt uneasy. They were wearing sheer low-cut dresses as they usually did on special occasions. Besides, it was August and very hot. But that kind of attire is strictly forbidden by Islamists. Fearing some unexpected reaction from Ahmed, they immediately put on their headscarves.[5] Those among us who still had doubts about the transformation Ahmed had undergone were now convinced—I being the first. Despite my disappointment, I put on a beautiful dress, as do all brides, and began to wait. I didn't quite know what to think. I noticed that the women in his family seemed surprised by my behavior. They knew Ahmed's way of thinking and found my attitude counter to Islamist norms. Then Houria, one of his cousins who considered herself more devout than the others, arrived. "You are no longer to wear short dresses," she said in an authoritative tone. "Or color your hair. Or put on makeup." Later I found out Houria was working with the "group." She also chastised me for having woven the design of a bird into the rug I had made especially for my new house. "You have sinned by representing a living creature," she told me. "On judgment day, that bird will demand that you give it life." I have to admit she succeeded in making an impression me. I started asking myself deep questions. Ones I couldn't answer.

Later that evening, my mother-in-law came to greet me. It was customary in their family for the bride to keep her veil over her face after arriving at the house until one of the groom's brothers lifted it. I would have waited forever because, after the trouble there had been between our two families, Ahmed's brothers were against the marriage, too. One of their uncles had to lift the veil instead. When my mother-in-law brought me coffee, my mother was afraid she might be trying to put a spell on me, given the bad state of mind all my in-laws were in, so my mother drank it for me.

Ahmed didn't arrive till very late. He was wearing a suit and a burnoose one of his friends who had gotten married the week before had lent him. Ahmed admitted he had hesitated between what he was wearing and what is prescribed by Islamist tradition: a *kamis*, kohl around the eyes, teeth whitened with *siwak*, hair greased with olive oil, and henna on the hands and feet.[6] They claim that's the way the prophet Muhammad dressed. "Since you never saw me done up like that before, I thought it might frighten you, so I put on a regular suit," he said. Then he asked me pointblank: "Did you recite the *Dhor* prayer?"[7] Of course I hadn't. To gain my composure, I started to laugh, and then thought of a ploy to get out of it: "Look! I'm wearing nail polish. Women aren't allowed to pray with nail polish on. You know that." He looked me up and down severely: "If you didn't say the Dhor, then you didn't say the *Asr* prayer either.[8] You're unclean. And this is how you present yourself to me?" We were getting off to a good start. Realizing this was not the kind of welcome to give his new bride, he got a hold of himself and spoke more gently: "The nail polish doesn't matter. You have an excuse. It's your wedding day. You can recite the prayer with it on." I told him sheepishly that what bothered me the most was going out into the yard to perform my ablutions. I might ruin my makeup. He thought of a solution: "You can use a stone to do your ablutions."[9] I complied. Then he took his place in front of me and we prayed together. The prayer lasted almost two hours. It seemed endless. I could hardly go on. When it was over, I felt exhausted. My knees hurt and my head was spinning. That was how the "brothers" prayed.

But it wasn't over yet. After the prayers he picked up the Koran from the nightstand and asked me to read him passages. I had had it! I wanted to throw the book in his face. I really thought he was making fun of me. When I realized he was serious, a tremendous feeling of sadness came over me. I started having depressing thoughts: other women got to listen to music, dance, and be happy on their wedding day, but I had to pray and read the Koran. I was too tired to resist though. I read a couple of verses, then stopped, determined to walk out on him on the spot if he said a word to me. After all, my parents' house was little more than thirty yards away. I was worn out and it was really late. He probably noticed my frustration, because he said: "You must be tired. Maybe you'd like to go to sleep." We finally went to bed. I had been waiting for that moment for so long. But it didn't last long. Ahmed got up and left before dawn. On his way out he said: "When I get back, you'd better have lunch ready for my 'brothers' and me."

8

My wedding night left me with a bitter feeling. I'd been saying my prayers regularly for a few years without being told. And I was more or less religious, although not excessively so. But in all honesty, I had never imagined I'd be spending my wedding night praying. What I'd been told by my girlfriends who got married before me had led me to hope for something different. That's why I was more than disappointed the next morning when Ahmed ordered me to prepare lunch for him and his brothers as he was leaving. I was really puzzled. Regardless, I still wanted to believe that the things I found shocking were unimportant details. I tried to get out of making lunch by saying that I was tired because we'd gone to bed so late. "I don't want to hear about it," he responded coldly. "You have to do it. Otherwise my brothers will make fun of me and say I married a lazy good-for-nothing." Since I knew he was a boaster, I actually believed he was asking me to do it so he could brag to his friends about me. I soon learned that preparing meals was first and foremost a duty. It was that overzealousness in carrying out missions for the GIA that later got Ahmed promoted to the rank of emir.

That night, he told me about his brothers and what they expected of me: "Now that we're married, you're part of the clan. You've become a sister. It's your obligation to cook for them and do their laundry. It will be your way of contributing to the creation of an Islamic state in Algeria. Somebody has to do those chores. The brothers are fighting against the taghout. God has ordered them to. And you have to help them find the strength to do it. Besides, anyone who supports them is also indirectly taking part in the fight. I want you to be the one to

x

37

help. That way, when I become an emir, you'll have the title of 'mother of the faithful' and God will count you among the chosen of the earth."[1] He managed to convince me. It wasn't long before I was accepting everything he said. According to him all Muslims had been unhappy since the abolition of the caliphate.[2] It needed to be reestablished in order to restore their happiness. "Mujahideen the world over are working to make it happen.[3] The GIA will see to it that the caliphate is reestablished in Algeria first. Once we have an Islamic state here, we'll liberate Palestine. They've been at war with the Jewish occupiers for years. We can't count on the taghout leading the Arab countries right now to liberate them. But, one by one, those very same Arab countries will be forced to set up Islamic regimes. After that, they'll all merge into one single nation. Then we'll conquer our enemies in the rest of the world." He said Algeria had to be purged of all the corrupt leaders in power who were crushing the people. "We'll exterminate all the big shots," he said. Ahmed would always use a proverb to prove his point: "You have to eat a bunch of grapes one grape at a time." The first ones who should be eliminated, he claimed, were the military—there were very few "patriots" then, and not many people in the villages had weapons. "Next it'll be the journalists' turn. We have to get rid of them all, and all the intellectuals, too, because anyone who's educated can use that knowledge to fight us. After that, we'll kill everybody in key positions and all their relatives. It's the only way we'll be able to impose the caliphate. Then we'll live the way they do in the soap operas on TV."

What he was saying was a bit frightening, but I admit I found it had a certain appeal. Killing all those people struck me as far too excessive, but the idea of one day living the way you see in the soaps was enticing. Still, I had to ask myself: how could the GIA govern without any intellectuals? I was sure they couldn't. What proved it was that the Islamists had a large segment of the population on their side in the beginning, but because of their ignorance they weren't able to hold on to those sympathizers. They did a lot of things people didn't approve of, or simply couldn't understand—like burning schools. Their motive was to do away with learning in Algeria so that everyone would be just as ignorant as they were. But I don't think Algerians want their children to be totally uncultivated. People strongly opposed burning the schools, especially since the ones targeted were those that poor children attended, not the ones in wealthy neighborhoods. The terrorists justified their actions by saying they were against teaching the way it was being done because it didn't give enough importance to the Koran and Islam, and it encouraged girls to be immoral: they wore pants and let their hair hang loose and blow in the wind. Islamic extremists want girls to wear headscarves. Early on, they coined a slogan that quickly spread throughout the neighborhoods they infiltrated: "Cover your hair and your earrings. Otherwise you'll face our *mahchoucha*."[4] Once the women heard this, none of them set foot outside without their headscarves again—not even little girls. Those who dared defy the order paid dearly, as did their parents. Take Katia, for example. She refused to wear a head-scarf. They slit her throat at school while her classmates and teacher watched. News of her fate quickly made its way to all the surrounding villages.

And so, the day after my wedding I assumed my new function: official cook for the GIA "group" in Hai Bounab.

9

My new task consisted of preparing all the meals: breakfasts, lunches, dinners. Sometimes there would be a fourth meal at night when the brothers were up late keeping watch. Every meal had to be a feast. There were always ten or twelve brothers at the table, but not always the same ones. They rotated, depending on their operations in the area. I knew a few of them, but when they were at the house, I wasn't allowed to stay and talk to them. I could only watch from behind a curtain, and if any of them wanted to say something to me, they had to turn their back to me. Their code of conduct prohibits them from looking at the wife of any member of the group, even if her head is covered. I'd stand by the door on occasion and listen to their conversation, but I did it in secret. Once, I lifted the curtain to see what those men were like who were making everyone tremble with fear. There before me stood a man so tall and strong that I was awed by the sight of him. When he looked at me, it was as though a light illuminated his face. He was so handsome! I was flustered to such an extent that I had to tell my husband about it. Naturally he gave me a stern lecture. He didn't like the fact that I was spying on his brothers, and liked even less that I was listening to their conversations.

My job consisted solely of preparing meals for them, and believe me, they didn't deprive themselves of anything. Greedy swine is what they were. For breakfast they had scrambled eggs with melted cheese. The eggs couldn't be overcooked or else "they'll lose their vitamins," Ahmed used to tell me. At first, I didn't know how to cook them the way the brothers liked, so Ahmed showed me. And there was hot milk—only the pure natural kind supplied by my mother-in-law, who raised cows. Some of the other neighbors did the same. They were only too happy to bring over several quarts each morning. There were toast rusks slathered with butter and jam—and fresh bread that some of the neighbors baked at dawn especially for them. I was the one who had to spread the butter and jam on the rusks to spare them every ounce of effort. They wanted to save their energy for the "great fight" and claimed they needed all that food to give them "the strength to combat the taghout." And to endure cold and hunger, if need be. But that wasn't all they ate. They demanded a traditional dish each morning. It varied according to the day: *mhadjeb, rfis, tamina, khouchkhach,* or *maarek.*[1] Making those dishes takes a lot of time. I'd start the night before and would wake up every morning before sunrise to finish so that everything would be out and ready the moment the brothers got up. It took me at least two hours. It was hard work, and I wasn't used to getting up so early. But what choice did I have?

Ahmed planned the menus for lunch and dinner. He bought the ingredients and sometimes showed me how to prepare dishes my mother hadn't taught me to make (we used to eat simple country food at our house). Otherwise, I'd go ask a neighbor how it was done. I learned quickly, but the most difficult thing to master was gauging the portions. For meat dishes, I had to cook mutton—a quarter or even half of the animal, along with all the vegetable accompaniments, of course. When they had chicken, I never cooked fewer than six or seven. Ahmed brought them home alive from the neighbor's coop and took care of slitting their throats. Then I had to pluck and clean them myself. Fried potatoes had to be served with a tomato-garlic sauce and were often accompanied by merguez sausage. The brothers were also fond of tripe with gravy. Cleaning the four or five bellies that Ahmed brought home was an ordeal in itself—especially with no running water. But tripe wasn't enough. I had to make *chak-*

chouka, too, or something else.[2] The brothers were very picky. Even when tomatoes were served with vinaigrette dressing, they had to be peeled. As did the grilled red and green peppers they ate daily. I burned my hands every time. In addition to the main courses, they had to have several salads, not to mention appetizers. In short, the meals needed to be varied and copious. They liked fish, too, particularly sardines. On those days, I'd elicit the help of two or three other women and together we'd clean the twenty-five pounds or so of sardines it would take to feed the group. Then I'd bake the sardines in the oven or fry them in batter with a special stuffing. Obviously, the most difficult dishes to prepare were the traditional ones, because they require a certain amount of time, experience, and finesse. It was even worse during Ramadan. The brothers didn't fast, on the pretext that they were at war and the Koran "excuses soldiers in combat from the obligation of fasting." They nevertheless still demanded the special Ramadan meal: *chorba* and *bourek* with ground meat, or, for variety's sake, spinach and cheese.[3] When I made chicken with artichokes — one of their favorites — I had to spend hours peeling the artichokes. When I was done, my hands were black and nearly bleeding.

The pace was all the harder for me because the work was so new. When I lived at home, my mother did the cooking. I never had to. I complained to Ahmed a few times, mostly after I got pregnant. I tried to make him feel sorry for me by reminding him of my condition, but he'd invariably answer: "That's what marriage is all about." He often recited a proverb that said if a woman enjoys the pleasant aspects of married life, she has to accept the disagreeable ones as well. Basically, what counted most for him was what his brothers thought. There were times when I wondered if he hadn't married me just so the group would have a cook. He was merciless and uncompromising. Even worse, we always had an argument whenever the salt or spices even slightly exceeded the amount the recipe called for.

That happened a lot, at least in the beginning. My mother-in-law, who lived just a few yards away, stopped by from time to time. She categorically refused to help me but would taste the food and offer her opinion. She knew what her son liked. The new arrangement suited her quite nicely because, before, she and some of the others used to frequently have the group over for meals. Thanks to me, she was able to kill two birds with one stone: she was freed of that drudgery and was able to dispel any suspicions that might have hung over her other three sons.

When I married Ahmed, it was a godsend not only for the group but for many of the women in the neighborhood as well. From that moment on, I alone was responsible for the thankless task of meeting the group's culinary needs. Before that, the other residents of Hai Bounab did it on a rotating basis. Those who could afford it took care of everything. Those who weren't as well off only did the cooking and let the group buy the food. Every family made it a duty to invite them to their home. I can assure you there isn't a single house in the village where they didn't eat at least once. The people considered it an honor to have them over for lunch or dinner. And besides, it was a way of ensuring they'd be in the GIA's good graces. But after I married Ahmed, the group came only to my house.

Before me, there was another woman in the village who fed the group more frequently than the rest. She was a real activist and organized political meetings with other women at the mosque. She was married but had no children. Her husband had deserted her. He vanished one day and was never heard from again. Unlike her, he was not at all in favor of the GIA, and since he couldn't do anything about it, he decided to leave. She told everyone he was sick and tired of seeing his wife wearing a headscarf, even at home, and hearing her talk about nothing but God and religion. She was always out and about, mostly at the mosque, trying to indoctrinate other women. She told me a sobering story that illustrates how bold some of the women militants could be: one day she was out proselytizing as usual when the police surrounded the mosque. They'd been tipped off that a terrorist was hiding inside. She'd seen him go in. She slipped him a *djelbab* and sneaked him out surrounded by a group of women.[4] But the women had overlooked the fact that he was wearing men's shoes, and that caught the attention of the police, who arrested the terrorist. As for her, they hauled her off to the police station where she was given the beating of her life. She never forgot that incident and spoke of it proudly.

After a few weeks on that grueling schedule, I was drained. I didn't even have time to say my prayers anymore. I spent every waking moment at the stove. And by the end of the day, I'd just collapse. All I could think about was getting some sleep. One day I went to visit my parents. It was the first time since my wedding the month before. I described my daily routine to my father. He had already noticed how thin I'd become and how tired I looked. I told him I couldn't even sleep at night because my husband made me keep watch for him and his friends, and I had to be up before sunrise to begin another day of drudgery. My father's affection for me hadn't changed. And although he was saddened to see me in such a state, he had to admit his hands were tied: "What can I do to help you? Not a thing. You see how all the neighbors are friendly and obliging to them. My only option is to do the same." When he said that, I understood the extent of the terrorists' power over the village.

Later on, when the police came to interrogate the people in Hai Bounab, they all naturally denied ever having had anything to do with terrorists. But I know what went on. My husband used to bring me documents for safekeeping in the house, and I would read them. There was a list of everyone who was collaborating with the GIA and what his or her connection was. The group put everything in writing. Even when they decided to kill someone, they wrote it down.

10

Khali Rabah was the man responsible for bringing the GIA and terrorism to Hai Bounab, back in early 1994. I was at my uncles' in Cheraga when he, his brother, and his family moved into a house near ours, paid for by the GIA. They had been living in Algiers, and it was obvious from the way they looked and acted. But they were poor. They had distant relatives in Hai Bounab. Before their arrival, it was a quiet place and we never had any trouble. The first time the police ever came to the village was when a young boy named Nacer was murdered.

I met Khali Rabah's family the day I was married. His wife and daughter congratulated me, even though they didn't know me. That's how members of the GIA ingratiate themselves with people—by appearing friendly and considerate. I only saw Khali Rabah once, when I was visiting my parents a few months after I'd been sent to Cheraga. He was very tall and strong. Everyone in the village knew he was the emir of Hai Bounab. He was the one who bought the house where the group met every day to plan its moves.

Khali Rabah moved to our village because he'd been spotted in Algiers, and the GIA wanted him to "manage" things here. All matters concerning Hai Bounab had to be cleared with him. He settled disputes among the residents. They loathed involving people outside their tribe, like my father, in their private business. The first dispute the group dealt with, and the one that made their existence and power known to everyone, was Nacera's case. She was a young neighbor girl who got pregnant while having an affair with a married man from another village. In her eighth month her lover abandoned her and went into hiding at his family's house near Medea. He had no desire to marry her. After lodging an unsuccessful complaint in court, Nacera's parents decided to turn to Khali Rabah. He notified members of the GIA in Medea. They tracked down the fugitive and forced him to marry Nacera. The incident proved that her lover was more afraid of the GIA than of government authorities. It's a well-known fact that the GIA has no tolerance for disobedience. You have to comply; otherwise they kill you. Khali Rabah was gunned down by the police in July 1995 during a clash in an orchard near Boufarik.

The GIA brought its own law and order to Hai Bounab, as was the case everywhere it established roots. The French language could no longer be taught. Anyone who did received death threats. The majority of the teachers, mostly women, chose to acquiesce. When girls reached the age of nine, they couldn't go to school anymore and had to cover their heads when they went outside. If they didn't, they would bring shame to the village. They carried within them the seed of *fitna*, the GIA claimed.[1] My husband even made my little sister wear a headscarf—and she was only seven. Whenever she came over to sleep at our house, he'd wake her up at dawn for prayers. And when she went to school, he asked her to count the number of patriots and policemen and report back to him about everything she heard and saw concerning them. All the children were made to spy for the group. They knew a lot of things but didn't say a word, even when the police tried to coerce them to talk. The terrorists threatened to kill their parents if they revealed anything. And so they, too, kept silent.

Boys got along well with the GIA. Consequently, they were allowed to continue their schooling—at least until the terrorists burned down most of the schools in the remote villages. The youngest boys were eager to work for terrorists. They idealized them and saw them as powerful role models because they were the ones who set the rules and commanded the respect of the people. And they always had lots of money and wore nice clothes—except when they engaged in guerilla fighting. Then they had to dress differently. They drove fancy new cars that they confiscated from the rich. They "worked" on them and rigged them for car bomb attacks.

They got their money from racketeering. I saw the files on people they forced to pay a "revolution" tax. Everyone in the farming town nearby was paying it—some as much as a million dinars. They had to hand over their share after every harvest. Those who didn't have money gave what they could: blankets, mattresses, dishes, whatever. The GIA in turn provided material assistance to all the poor. I think some people cooperated with the group because they believed in what it was doing, but a lot did so out of fear. They were nice to my father. That was understandable. He didn't have anything to give them.

From what Ahmed told me, he decided to join the GIA the day he was arrested at the Mosque in Benramdane. He was there for the Friday services when the police surrounded the building and forced everyone to go outside. They hauled him down to the station along with others suspected of having links with terrorists. They were all beaten. Ahmed was locked up in a cell for three days and made to do disgusting chores, like clean the toilets. He told me that was the day he decided to join, to get back at the police. But I think he wanted to join much earlier, because he started reciting prayers and hanging around the group long before that. Besides, ever since I'd known him, he hated the police and anything related to the government. My family cried the day President Boudiaf was assassinated.[2] But Ahmed made no attempt to hide his joy, even though he had no interest in politics back then. He was just waiting for the right occasion to take the plunge. I think that's why Khali Rabah chose him over all the other young men in Hai Bounab to be part of the organization. He sensed that Ahmed was naturally predisposed to terrorism.

Actually, as soon as the group showed up in the village, they took an interest in Ahmed because he was such a daredevil and so aggressive. He liked to pick fights and never backed off. Another reason was that he knew Hai Bounab and the surrounding area like the back of his hand. But what they especially liked was that he was from Kef Lakhdar, the GIA stronghold in the Medea region. That was a very important location for the GIA. The groups in Algiers and on the Mitidja Plain had numerous ties with the ones there. When Khali Rabah found out Ahmed had spent his childhood in Kef Lakhdar and still had family in the vicinity, he suggested Ahmed work as an intermediary between Hai Bounab and Kef Lakhdar. Also in Ahmed's favor was the fact that he didn't have a police record yet, so he could move about freely. That's how he wound up being recruited, even though he'd never been an activist and hadn't taken an interest in religious issues before. In fact, he'd been far removed from such things. The change happened during our separation. Ahmed's way of thinking was completely turned around, and I know Khali Rabah was the one responsible, although Ahmed never wanted to admit it. I guessed it from the way Ahmed would talk to me about Khali Rabah after he died, the way he venerated the man who was twenty years his senior. Before making Ahmed part of the group, Khali Rabah managed to get him to go to the mosque regularly. Ahmed had never set foot in one before. It was a way of testing Ahmed's ability to discipline himself. Once they felt he had passed the test, they allowed him to join one of the commandos.

Ahmed's role in the beginning was to pass on information. After they decided he was trustworthy, they let him into their hideout and showed him how they operated, where they held their meetings, went under cover, and planned their maneuvers. It was an observation phase that all new recruits had to go through. Ahmed started by bringing them meals the neighbors prepared when the men didn't want to come out of hiding.

He ran errands for them that required going into Algiers and picking up items in department stores, specialty shops, or on the black market—especially clothes and all the paraphernalia specific to the GIA. The group bought him a motorbike to make getting around easier. When they weren't dressed in their traditional gear, group members wore nothing but the most expensive designer clothes: sweaters costing two thousand dinars, leather jackets that went for twenty thousand, and Reebok, Nike, or Fila running shoes at ten thousand dinars a pair. Ahmed said they had to wear good sport shoes so they could make a fast getaway if they had to.

Ahmed bought them a special ambergris-based cologne from Saudi Arabia, as well as *siwak*, henna, kohl, copies of the Koran, and propaganda books that he'd pick up in Algiers from black-market dealers. And pants, too—expensive jeans. They'd cut them off at the knees to adapt them to Islamist attire and to make it easier for them to run. Mostly, they wore wide Afghan-style pants, but some of them preferred jeans. They put on green or brown kamis over them. When they had to make a run for it, they pulled up the kamis and tucked them in their belts. Some wrapped long green or black scarves around their heads. It wasn't uncommon for them to get fabric and take it to seamstresses to have clothes made. The women were so afraid of the GIA, they never refused. In any case, they were well paid, so they didn't grumble much. The most style-conscious militants liked traditional loose-fitting pants with silk embroidery at the knees. According to GIA theorists, women should wear long dark dresses covering their arms, forearms, and neck. The dresses need to be big enough so as not to show the women's figures. Above all, women must avoid anything see-through or tight. I remember one day I was wearing a white blouse that was slightly transparent. It was very hot and the two of us were alone in the house, but Ahmed made me put something on over it just the same. The next day, he bought me a dress he had picked out himself. I didn't like at all, but it was in keeping with his standards. I had to wear it every day. He never let me take off my khimar in the house when I was alone with him, even in the middle of the summer.

Clearly Ahmed's functions could not remain limited to menial tasks. He became an important part of the group very quickly. But it was only after we were married that he got into guerilla fighting. Following Khali Rabah's death, the GIA members in Hai Bounab went without an emir for several months, during which they were under the sole authority of the *caïd*.[3] Then Ahmed took over. It was only logical. That happened in November of 1995, a few weeks before the presidential elections.

The day I was arrested, the police were surprised that I, the emir's wife, wasn't wearing jewelry like the others. I have to admit it flattered my ego knowing I was married to the leader.

11

Before they're allowed to join the insurgent forces up in the mountains, terrorists have to go through a probationary period. For months on end, the local leaders observe the behavior of every man who wants to be part of their contingent. They put both his loyalty to the GIA and his reliability to the test. There are some who willingly work for the group although they prefer to stay at home with their families. But even those men invariably end up joining the others, because sooner or later the security forces spot them and they don't feel safe in cities or towns anymore. And they always need more men in the mountains. Besides, the GIA never has complete confidence in activists until they've fought in combat. That's because once men have fought, their involvement is virtually irreversible. Even if they might later have regrets and want to get out, they'd have to face doing time in prison.

The brothers must have noticed how anxious Ahmed was to be part of the guerilla fighting. But he was reluctant to give up the comfort of his home and family. To push him over the line, they staged their usual scenario: one day they sent one of their men to my brother-in-law's. It was someone nobody in the village knew. He pretended to be from the security forces. "Rumor has it that your brother is a terrorist," he said to my brother-in-law, knowing full well he'd be worried and would rush to tell Ahmed. And that's exactly what he did. That evening, when Ahmed told me what had happened, I knew immediately it was a ploy by the group to force him to further commit himself to their cause. It was easy to see. If the military had really been after him, they'd have come directly to our house, as they had so many times before. But Ahmed got scared. "My brothers would never do anything like that to me," he said. He was convinced of it. Naturally, he told them the whole story. Far from reassuring him, they did everything they could to get him more worked up, and said the time had come for him to join their encampment in the mountains. Ahmed had no choice but to relent. He was very excited by the prospect, since carrying a weapon constantly had long been his dream, but he was a little uneasy. He knew what he'd be giving up and had no idea what he was getting into. His friends took him away somewhere for a week. I didn't hear from him the entire time. He came back two days before the presidential elections.

We'd been married three months, and I was a few days pregnant, although I didn't know it yet. I felt nauseous and couldn't figure out why. When Ahmed returned, he was a different man. He'd lost weight. He'd blackened his eyes with kohl, rubbed olive oil in his hair, and splashed himself with strong-smelling ambergris perfume. He was wearing a green kamis and had a long black scarf wrapped around his head. It was the first time he was dressed like "them." He had a mahchoucha slung over his shoulder. He jumped over the wall and came in through the window—as he always did. The figure I saw approach was totally unrecognizable. I was panic-stricken. After I got over the shock, I began sobbing. I suddenly realized I had lost him forever. It was as if he had died. Then he told me everything: he hadn't had anything to eat or drink the whole week he was up in the mountains. It was a test to measure his stamina for the hardships of life as a guerilla fighter. His body was covered with marks and bruises. They beat him over and over every day with all kinds of objects to see how well he endured physical pain. When I expressed surprise at their barbarism, he explained with unwavering conviction that they had to do it to determine if he could hold up under torture. They also taught him how to use weapons. He was awed by it all. As he was telling me everything he'd gone through, there was a kind of cheerfulness in his voice, even when he described being beaten. He was in ecstasy—especially when he talked about the weapons. He had long wanted to learn how to use them, but his brothers wouldn't show him. They kept saying: "Later. When we take you up to the encampment."

In the course of the three short months I spent with Ahmed, I learned a lot about the GIA's activities—even things he refused to tell me. All I had to do was watch. Ahmed often came home with his hands completely bruised. He said it was because the work he was doing was very hard. And it was. They dug bunkers, made bombs, and smuggled weapons they stole from the security forces and rigged for their own purposes. They learned how to do all that in the guerilla camps. Specialists with expertise in different areas came from other parts of the country to train them. That's how Ahmed learned to make bombs and booby-trap cars. They had him specialize in explosives because when he was very young he had learned the rudiments of electricity from one of his uncles, who was an electrician. Ahmed had repaired televisions and radios and one time even made a radio transmitter. The group picked people based on their experience. Once a man had been selected, he had to do as he was told, whether he liked it or not. He had no say in the matter. Otherwise either he or members of his family would be killed. They forced our neighbor, Saïd, to go into the wilds with them. He couldn't read or write. He just had a beautiful voice—the kind that's perfect for reciting the Koran. They made him live with them in the wilderness and brought children there so he could teach them how to recite the Koran. If I'm not mistaken, that's where he died. In the mountains.

Whenever I criticized Ahmed for not having steady work, he'd ridicule me: "What are you talking about? I'm fighting the great fight against the taghout. That job is more important and far more demanding than any other." But I also believe it was more profitable doing what he did than normal work would have been. So why should he switch? For the first few days after our wedding, Ahmed didn't sleep at home. He spent part of the evening with me, then would disappear in the middle of the night. He and his brothers would come back around dawn, in time for breakfast. I have no idea where he went. He refused to say, and always gave me the same answer when I asked him: "I have important work to do." It was only much later that I learned exactly what that "work" was—by putting together pieces of information that he gave me or I got from other sources.

After a month had gone by, the group began to feel at ease in my house. They liked it so much that they started sleeping there—at first in twos and threes. Then the number grew to ten or twelve. It was an invasion. I had no choice but to let them have the bedroom. I set up a cot in the kitchen for Ahmed and me. But the worst part about it was that I wasn't allowed to sleep when they spent the night at our house—which quickly became a habit. I had to keep watch. Ahmed gave all the blankets to his brothers and only let me cover myself with a lightweight sheet so that the cold night air would prevent me from falling into a deep sleep. After a month the brothers moved in permanently. That's when Ahmed decided to build an extra room to accommodate them. The yard was tiny. To make space for the room, he and his friends uprooted an old fig tree that had been planted right in the middle. The trunk was so big that when they removed it, it left an enormous gaping hole. They decided to make the hole even bigger and turn it into a hiding place. They told me to go to my mother's—to get rid of me. The digging went on all day. Once the hideout was finished, they set a stone slab over it, leaving an opening for access, and put up the walls of the room.

12

I had to go along with everything that happened in my house. There was no alternative. Ahmed kept telling me: "We have to show the brothers hospitality, otherwise they'll be forced to sleep out in the cold and God will punish us both." I was terribly afraid of divine punishment. Their big fear, on the other hand, was being caught off guard by the police. It was so bad that they slept with their clothes on, including their running shoes (which they never took off). That way, if they were awakened in the middle of the night and needed to make a quick escape, they'd be ready. Once in a while I had Ahmed remove his shoes. When he did, a nauseating stench filled the room. It made me sick to my stomach. It was no use trying to get him to take a shower, but I'd ask him to at least wash his feet now and then. Actually, I was the one who washed them, because he claimed he already had enough tiring work to do. Besides, I should participate in the good deeds he was performing. He maintained that when a man wages jihad, God credits half the deeds to the man's wife.[1] That's why whenever he came home and found me lying down resting—which was rare, I must say—he ordered me to get up immediately. "There's no reason I should wear myself out while you reap half the benefits without doing anything," he exclaimed on those occasions. Washing his feet for him was therefore an act of devotion to God.

And so was washing their clothes. Ahmed regularly brought home large bags full of dirty laundry. Since we didn't have running water in the house, I'd go to the well with five-gallon containers. I used to pile them onto a wheelbarrow so I could get all the water in one trip. When I put the dirty clothes in the hot water, lice came out by the dozens and floated to the top. I could barely stand it when I was pregnant. I often vomited while doing the laundry, but I knew I had to finish the work. Otherwise I'd be subjected to another of Ahmed's reprimands. And I did it willingly because I truly believed I was making my own modest contribution to the great cause of reestablishing the caliphate on Islamic soil. My husband used to say that the more we suffer when working for the mujahideen, the more God is pleased with us. Sometimes it took me an entire day and several boxes of detergent to get those clothes looking clean. On laundry day, they knew they couldn't count on me to make a huge meal for them. They had to make do with omelets and fried potatoes.

That's how I spent my days—toiling constantly. I was so tired at night that I couldn't keep my eyes open, despite everything my husband did to prevent me from falling asleep. Needless to say, I had little time for leisure or amusement of any kind. Besides, after Ahmed joined the GIA, he avoided anything and everything that might put us in a good mood. When I first met him, he was so fun-loving, but after we were married I saw him smile or laugh only on a few rare occasions, with his brothers. Not with me. He wouldn't even let me listen to Radio Koran, which only broadcasts religious songs (but set to pleasant music).[2] If he came home unexpectedly and heard the radio, he'd lose his temper and turn it off right away. More than once, Ahmed came close to breaking the radio because of that. The only thing he liked was sadness. "Joy is for later," he said. "Until the Islamic state has been set up, there's no reason to celebrate."

He had a theory for every daily activity, no matter how mundane it might be. When drinking a glass of water, you pick up the glass with your right hand and take three small sips before drinking the rest. You should never eat too much—just enough for the hunger to subside. You should always be sure you feel slightly hungry. That rule was for other people, though. He and his brothers never followed it themselves. They had an excuse: they could eat like hogs "to have the strength to fight the taghout." And there was a special prayer to be said before entering the bathroom. When we were in bed, we put out the lights and weren't supposed to disrobe completely. I only saw my husband naked once. I went into the bedroom unexpectedly while he was getting undressed. He was furious. "You've just committed a sin. We have to cover ourselves in front of God," he shouted. Before touching me in bed, he always recited this prayer: "In the name of God, keep Satan far from us and from everything Thou might give us." In other words, he was asking God to keep Satan from coming between us, and also to keep him away from the child that might be born of our union. Even when I was pregnant, he made sure to recite that prayer when he got into bed. He used to say that, without such rituals, human existence would be barbaric.

As far as politicians were concerned, he didn't care for any of them, with the exception of Abdallah Djaballah.[3] Ahmed said that there'd be no need for political parties in an Islamic state. All we'd have to do is follow the Koran and the Sunna.[4] He hated Mahfoud Nahnah.[5] He considered him the biggest taghout of all because he gave women too many rights. He thought Abassi Madani was just "a dirty traitor and a taghout trying to get a seat in the government."[6] Ahmed was convinced that the only way to build an Islamic state was through bloody combat and the physical elimination of all adversaries. The political figure he hated the most was unquestionably Liamine Zeroual, the president of Algeria. One day rumors spread that he'd been shot at but had escaped injury. Ahmed was disappointed. He kept saying: "That dog. He may be strong today, but we'll get him in the end. His day will come, too. Like the others."

In 1995 everyone in our village voted in the November 16 presidential election. Everyone except me. Ahmed wouldn't let me. "They're all a bunch of taghout," he said. The day before the election, he brought home almonds and chocolates and ate them with his friends but told me I couldn't have any. He cited one of his many bizarre theories—one that was only applicable to me: "If you get in the habit of nibbling, that's all you'll think about and you'll forget about God." We had a big fight that night, partially because I was tired of having him deprive me of so many things he indulged in himself. But also because he didn't want me to vote. My mother had me get a voting card, and he wasn't letting me use it. The day of the election, I gathered my things together in the morning and told him I was walking out on him. Seeing how determined I was, he thought I was serious. When I was about to leave, he started to cry, then said: "If you want your card stamped, I can do it. I've got a stamp." A rumor had been going around for a few days that people would need their voting cards to be able to get any kind of legal paperwork. People whose cards hadn't been stamped at a polling station would be suspected of supporting the GIA. My foremost concern was having my child's birth officially registered. But Ahmed was inflexible. "In any case, we're going to set up an Islamic state soon, and you won't need papers from those heathens."

In the days preceding the election, Ahmed went around try-ing to convince the residents of Hai Bounab not to vote. He and his group even slapped a warning on the walls: "Today it's votes, tomorrow it will be bullets, and after that, the walls will be covered with blood." The people were afraid of what the GIA might do, but they voted just the same. They were hesitant in the beginning. Everyone was watching everyone else. No one wanted to go first. Then, once a few were bold enough to head to the polling stations, the rest followed their example. The strangest thing was that by the afternoon all of them were proudly showing off their voting cards, duly stamped. In the end there wasn't any trouble on either side. I'm convinced the terror-ists didn't punish the people in our village because they needed them. That was when they still knew how to stay within bounds.

13

When Ahmed became the emir of the group, which was soon after the guerilla camp became his base, he explained to me that his organization was called the GIA and that its leader was someone by the name of Antar Zouabri. [1] Ahmed talked about him as though he were some supernatural being. "The military can look for him all they want, they'll never find him," he told me. [2] "They imagine him living in a palace, but he's a man of the people. He lives like everyone else. He eats with us, sleeps with us, and does what we do." Ahmed told me that all the GIA members knew Zouabri because he visited each local group regularly. But as a rule it was the local emirs, especially from the Matidja region, who went to see him to report on their operations. They usually met in Douar Lahdjar and Ouled Allel, their biggest strongholds. [3] When Ahmed first told me about Ouled Allel, I didn't pay much attention. I really didn't know what was going on there. I only found out after I was free and started reading the papers. While I was with him, he didn't allow me to do that. Antar Zouabri was the one who appointed each local emir and his right-hand man, the caïd. He also settled any disputes that might arise between them and, most essential of all, distributed the war booty among the various groups and local emirs. But I can attest to the fact that he never gave us anything. My husband collected the booty himself during operations he led in his own zone of action. And after my husband disappeared, I never received a cent.

Whenever Ahmed talked to me about his activities, his intent was to change my mindset. And he succeeded. Little by little, I started to do everything he told me without complaining.

Perhaps partly out of fear—after he described all the atrocities he'd inflicted on others—and partly because he managed to convince me that their cause was just, even to the point where I didn't question some of the punishments he subjected me to, like the *falaqa*.[4] One day I committed what was considered an offense. The brothers were in the yard by the house and, although I wasn't supposed to, I went to see what they were doing. My husband caught me spying on them and decided to beat me on the back with a leather whip. In theory, he could give me up to forty lashes, but seeing I was in great pain—even though I suffered in silence and never let out a single sound—he took pity on me and only gave me ten.

Another time, Ahmed subjected me to the falaqa because I was listening to music on the radio. The precepts of the GIA stipulate that the only recordings a believer can listen to are passages from the Koran—never joyful songs. "You must always be ready for judgment day," he would say. I was home alone that day and was bored, so I turned on the radio. He came back unexpectedly. As soon as I saw him coming, I turned it off. He noticed I was in a good mood and wanted to know why I was so perky. I told him it was the radio. He was furious and gave me the falaqa because I'd broken one of the rules. That day, I got thirty lashes.

Ahmed said he wasn't fighting just the taghout. He was battling demons, too—jinn: "There are too many jinn in our country. We need to eradicate them from society. Purify it once and for all." I think he was right. In my family alone, there are three women possessed by demons. They've entered the women's bodies and won't leave them. My husband would say: "You see? We have to fight on several fronts. First of all, against this heathen government; next, against the traitors; and last, against the jinn." I remember an incident involving one of Ahmed's closest friends, Rachid. He'd been engaged to his cousin since childhood. They grew up together. He didn't love her, but she was crazy about him. When Rachid was killed, his fiancée became possessed by a jinn. Her aunt called on Ahmed and his friends for help. They locked themselves in a room with her and recited verses from the Koran. It seems that as soon as she heard them, she went into a trance and took off all her clothes. After two or three more sessions, she was completely cured. Ahmed told me that during the exorcism, it was he who would turn into a demon. He was therefore the one who had taken possession of the woman.

I'd never been possessed by a jinn, but Ahmed put me through the same type of exorcism. Whenever I got really edgy, he'd recite verses from the Koran into a glass of water and make me drink it. I felt calmer right away. Ahmed learned the Koran when he was little, but later forgot it. It came back to him when he began associating with the Islamists. He always said that women are highly susceptible to demonic possession, that they need to be closely monitored and put on the path of righteousness very early. That's why he and the others sought out adulteresses and stoned them. They killed several that way. Or else they tortured and mutilated them with a knife. They didn't do that in our village. There weren't any bad women there. The only ones they didn't like were the five girls they decapitated. The terrorists took their cues on how to behave from the teachings of a little book called *Hosn El Muslim*.[5] It explains how good Muslims should conduct themselves in life.

Killing was always on their minds. I was lying on the floor one day when a rat scurried by. I jumped up and screamed. Ahmed was there and heard me. "How can you be afraid of a rat?" he asked in surprise. "I'll show you how to attack it." He knocked it unconscious with a shoe, then told me: "Come and kill it yourself." The very idea terrified me. But he insisted, and even threatened to hit me if I didn't do as he said. The only rationale he could come up with to persuade me was: "This is how you learn to kill. First a rat, then a human." He wanted to teach me to kill at any cost. He talked about it repeatedly. Once, before he went up into the mountains, he took a mahchoucha that belonged to one of his "brothers." He brought it home to show me how to load and unload it. While he was demonstrating, he did something wrong and it went off. The bullet hit the wall. When his friends found out what happened, they punished him—both for stealing the weapon and for his clumsiness. He was the one who got the falaqa that time. They tied him to a tree and gave him several blows on his back and the bottom of his feet.

One day Ahmed came home with a woman. Her name was Hadda. All he told me when he dropped her off was that she was going to be staying with us. She was five months pregnant and had the flu to boot. She was from Constantine. I couldn't speak their language yet, so when he introduced me to her using words I didn't know, I thought he'd taken her as a second wife.[6] She was very pretty. He left her there with me and went off somewhere. After that she didn't say a word—it's a rule among terrorists and their families never to utter a sound in front of strangers. She was waiting for her husband to tell her how she should interact with me and to what extent she could trust me. Ahmed returned that evening with his friends. His arms were weighed down with groceries for dinner. It had to be something special that night, he said, in honor of Hadda. I was still wondering what was going on but didn't dare say anything. When he asked me to prepare the bedroom for her, I was sure the room was for him too. I was brokenhearted, but I did as he said. While I was making the bed, he came into the room. I couldn't put off asking the question that had been gnawing at me any longer. Flattered by my jealousy, he burst out laughing and reassured me: "She's our brother Karim's wife. They're going to be reunited here tonight in our house. They've been separated for months." Karim and his two brothers had been wanted terrorists for a long time. Hadda and Karim spent a week with us then left. He went back to join the guerilla fighting, and I don't know where she went. That's how she lived—going from house to house, or even town to town, to meet up with her husband because he couldn't stay in one place more than a week at a stretch.

When she arrived Hadda locked herself in a silence that I thought was needlessly exaggerated, but she came out of it as soon as her husband told her she could trust me. The first comment she made was a criticism. In her view I wasn't militant enough. "You have to help the brothers wage jihad to reestablish the caliphate," she told me. "We women can do a lot to attain that noble objective." She told me she organized meetings with other "sisters." I let her know she was the first sister under my roof, and seeing as how I spent the entire day every day in front of the stove, I didn't have time for endless discussions. At first she tried to set an example for me. She wanted to give me the impression she was a strong and determined woman. But once we were both on the same wavelength, she dropped her mask and admitted she wasn't as happy with her situation as she had wanted me to believe. She even said she envied me because I'd had a real civil wedding service and I had a home with my husband. She, on the other hand, had had a bogus wedding—just a religious ceremony in front of the brothers. It wasn't legal, and she was forced to wander from town to town to see her husband. Sometimes she went four or five months at a time without seeing him. She was especially saddened by the thought that the child she was carrying would be registered on public records as born of an unknown father and an unwed mother. When the child reached school age, it would be an even greater problem. Hadda's sister was married to a terrorist as well. The two sisters had married two brothers.

I saw Hadda again four months later. She was nine months pregnant, and her husband had just been killed. With no father and no identity, children of terrorists are doomed to hardship all their lives. But their mothers weren't thinking about that when they got married. They believed the Islamists would take over. And back then, terrorists at least took the trouble to lawfully marry women. Now they take them by force, gang rape them, then kill them. And hack up their bodies.

14

Ahmed didn't tell me everything, because I was quick to voice my disapproval of excessive violence. But when he was in a good mood and I bombarded him with questions, he described some of the terrorist acts he had committed with his brothers. On days when he came home beaming with joy, I knew they had carried out some murderous attack. "Victory over the taghout is on its way," he'd say triumphantly.

I know, for example, that they were behind the death of the young man who helped my father get a job at the town hall. He was a terrific boy—friendly, polite, and well liked. He'd gone off to do his military service. Three months before it was over, he was granted leave to visit his parents. The very day he arrived in Hai Bounab, the terrorists pressured him to go up to their encampment with them. He refused—he was religious but opposed terrorism. So in the middle of the night, they surrounded his parents' house and kidnapped him. We didn't get any news of him for a long time. After I was married I asked Ahmed if he knew what had happened. He told me he'd been killed in Maassouma, near Blida, along with about forty other terrorists. They were bombarded by an army helicopter.

One day Ahmed gloated as he told me the story of one of his friends living in Eucalyptus who used to stop by our house occasionally. He killed his own brother for answering the draft call and joining the army. That was the only reason. He was on leave visiting his family one day when, as chance would have it, he ran into his terrorist brother, who slit his throat in front of their mother. She nearly went insane.

In a nearby village the terrorists killed a farmer because he refused to give them his hunting rifle. He had been denounced by his own son. The day they came to confiscate his weapon, the farmer staunchly denied owning one. They searched the house, found nothing, and left. But later the man's son assured them that his father did indeed own a gun and told them where it was hidden. To prove he wasn't lying, he went with them to his father's and helped them find it. The terrorists slit the man's throat in front of his son, who was then proclaimed a hero.

Young Nacer's murder was the first in Hai Bounab. He was fifteen years old. His only mistake was hanging around with patriots. All the villagers were under strict orders never to speak to them — and everyone obeyed. But Nacer liked to make small talk with them in front of their headquarters. One night, the terrorists went to his parents' house and asked to be served dinner. Their hosts complied, of course. After they'd stuffed themselves, they got up from the table and asked Nacer to follow them outside. He was standing in the doorway when they shot him in the head. Nacer was buried the following day, and no one made any attempt to file a complaint with the police. That was one year before I was married, but I know Ahmed was among the terrorists who did it. Nacer's mother told me so later.

At least it can be said that, because it was so quick, Nacer's death was relatively painless. Others suffered horribly before they died. One day the terrorists stopped a policeman in an orchard. "What kind of work do you do?" they asked. He couldn't lie because they had found an ID card on him that proved he worked for the police. But he tried to get out of it by saying, "I'm just a cook." It was the wrong thing to say. "Oh, so you're the one who fattens the pigs?" they laughed. No matter what he had answered, he wouldn't have escaped the fate awaiting him. They "had some fun with him," to use my husband's expression. They started by poking out one of his eyes with a rusty metal wire they found on the ground. "We'll leave the other one in so you can see what we're going to do to you," they said, still laughing. Then they chopped him up, starting with his toes and fingers. They cut them off one by one and hacked his entire body into little pieces. Ahmed roared with laughter as he told me the story.

But I have to say, too, that some take advantage of terrorism to get even with people they don't like. There was this rich man who regularly gave large sums of money to the GIA. He owned a factory that manufactured construction materials and used to shell out up to 500,000 dinars a month to the terrorists. One day, when a group of armed men showed up for the money, he asked them to wait, slipped out the back door, and called the police, then ran back and started talking with them as if it were business as usual. The police soon arrived and arrested the men. The group never suspected that the industrialist had anything to do with it. Since the terrorists couldn't come by to extort money from him, he had some peace and quiet for a while. But a few months later, he and an associate bought a piece of land with the intention of reselling it. When it came time to sell, they had a disagreement. The associate felt he'd been hoodwinked. To get even, he told the terrorists that his partner was the one who had turned their friends in. They went to the industrialist's home, kidnapped him, cut his body into pieces, then spread them on the ground in front of his house.

Terrorists have no pity and never forgive anybody anything. As soon as they have the slightest doubt about someone, they kill him without ever bothering to check if their suspicions are justified or not. And it goes without saying that they never take extenuating circumstances into account, no matter how loyal the person they have doubts about may have been until then. Such was the case of Djamel. He had been one of them. His job was to collect money in Hai Bounab and from the farmers in the area then turn it over to either the emir or the caïd. One day the group decided to kill him. They based their decision solely on the fact that someone had told them he was planning to leave the group and turn them in. At least that's what they claimed. But others say Ahmed and two of his friends stole the money Djamel had collected and killed him so he couldn't talk.

The brothers' cruelty knew no limits. Neither did their cynicism. They had so much blood on their hands they couldn't keep things in perspective anymore. Once, they killed a young woman in Baba Ali because she was engaged to a policeman. She had gold fillings in her teeth. When Ahmed got home, he said: "I wanted to pull out the gold and bring it home for you, but I didn't have time." He betrayed no emotion when he told me that. It was the most natural thing in the world to him. I shuddered, realizing he had no idea how disgusted I was by the very idea. But I was careful not to tell him.

While Ahmed and I were living together, he never executed anyone himself. That's what he led me to believe, anyway, because his specialty was making bombs. Later, I learned that he took part in the killings and even enjoyed it. But I know there was a designated killer in their group whose job it was to torture people and slit their throats when the leader ordered him to. The killer was a boy of fifteen, with a slight build. Before he committed the murders, the group gave him drugs—either by injections or pills. Ahmed told me the boy had seen his four brothers, all terrorists, killed in a skirmish with the military. During that same operation, a helicopter bombed their house and killed their mother. Her body was crushed under the rubble. He was the only one in the family who escaped. After that he turned heartless, devoid of any emotion. He dreamed of nothing but violence. All he thought about was getting even. He used to come over to our house from time to time. He dressed the way they did, with a green kamis and a long scarf around his head, and he talked like an old man. He was full of hate.

Both the police and the patriots do shocking things sometimes, too. Especially the patriots. Like the time I was at the bus station in Benramdane, waiting for the transport van to pick us up. I saw the patriots dragging the body of a man they had tied to the back of a truck. He was completely naked except for a piece of paper covering his penis. He had a beard and long hair. The patriots dragged his body around the entire village, shouting for joy. The villagers applauded. The people waiting for the van scattered, some out of fear, and others to get a better view. I was left standing there, all alone. I broke down in tears at the thought that the same thing could happen to my husband.

I was appalled when Ahmed told me about the atrocities he and his group committed. Every time he did, I imagined he was capable of doing something similar to me—or to someone in my family. I'd stare at his hands and think: "How many people have those hands killed?" And I became increasingly afraid of him, because I knew that, although he loved me, he was merciless. I'm convinced that if he'd ever had the slightest doubt about me, I would not have been spared. Still worse, I'd have been subjected to the special treatment reserved for traitors. Betraying the cause is worse than a crime for them. It calls for the strongest form of punishment. What they do to the taghout is nothing by comparison. Ahmed even said that if his mother or brother ever committed an offense, he wouldn't hesitate to punish them himself. So you can imagine what he would have done to me, the "mother of the faithful"!

15

Ahmed's job was to make bombs and rig them up to cars manned by suicide bombers. The day of the operation, a very precise ritual was performed to prepare the driver. He was made up the way the dead are before burial. The group rubs henna on the bomber's hands, he's expected to whiten his teeth with siwak, and so on. "So they'll look their finest when they appear before God," they said. Ahmed was very tempted by the idea of committing suicide in one of their operations, but he didn't want to do it alone. He asked me once if I'd like to go with him. We'd drive off together in a car loaded with explosives and both die. He tried to get me to say yes by telling me it was the supreme act of devotion. I refused. I didn't want to die. The suicide mission he was talking about would have been an attack on the police station in either Eucalyptus or Baraki.

Another time he came up with a different way for me to sacrifice my life. His plan was to plant a bomb at the front door of our house with wires leading outside so that I could set it off after luring the police or the patriots there. The bomb would blow up the house, the police, and me. Again, I said no. When I told my parents about Ahmed's deadly plans, they were stunned: "Is that all he wants for you? Death?" I really think he wanted to see me die. Preferably before he did, because he knew he didn't have long to live. Several of his friends had died in suicide bombings.

As far as making bombs went, I know he was quite involved in it. I could always tell when he was making them because he came home tired and jittery. He said it required a great deal of concentration. And he was on edge until he found out if they had achieved the desired effect. He never made bombs at the house. Mostly he made them in Ouled Allel, where the group had a laboratory. At night they planned where bombs would be planted, especially the ones targeting military convoys. I used to watch members of the group take shovels and pickaxes from the house and go off to dig holes and bury the devices. Ahmed was in charge of the Hai Bounab area and some of the neighboring villages. Every area had its own explosives specialist, so Ahmed didn't make bombs intended for Algiers. When the results were good, that is, when they killed a lot of people, he was very pleased.

One day they planted a high-caliber bomb in front of the hospital in Benramdane, right near a police station. It killed about ten policemen and patriots. Ahmed was happier than I'd ever seen him — even happier than on our wedding day, which had taken place only a few days earlier. Among the dead was a man whose wife I knew quite well. She was a wonderful woman and the mother of two children. When I ran into her several months after the attack, she told me in all frankness: "Your husband killed mine, but I don't hold it against you because I can see you're just as unhappy as I am. He'll be the cause of his son's misfortune, too. You and I are innocent victims." Her words broke my heart. I believe that at that moment I hated Ahmed.

Another time Ahmed planted a bomb on a road to Eucalyptus that the military convoy took daily. He planned for it to explode when the convoy was passing by, but it went off before it was supposed to, barely a few minutes after he'd set it in the hole. Some soldiers patrolling the area spotted him and figured he had done it. They chased him through the orchards but were unable to capture him. The bomb didn't kill anyone, but it left a huge crater in the middle of the road. Since they couldn't get Ahmed, the police came and nabbed his brother instead. That evening Ahmed stormed into the house, scribbled a note, and threw it out in the yard to me. I was out there talking with some women from next door. Then he left as quickly as he'd come in. In his note he told me to leave the house for a few days and hide out with my maternal uncles until his brother was released. He was afraid his brother would give my name to the police. I did what he said and was gone for three days. His brother was detained for forty-eight hours then discharged. Ahmed disappeared for a week. Later, two of his brothers were killed at the exact same spot where he'd planted the bomb intended for the military.

The last bomb to explode in Hai Bounab was the one that went off at the school. The terrorists had decapitated those five girls the night before. In the course of his investigation the next morning, the captain of the Eucalyptus police squad came to my parents' house to find out where I was. He questioned my mother and brother, then went by the school to see if I was there. They were the last people to talk to him. There was a GIA propaganda tract on the school wall. It was a trap. The tract covered a hole where a bomb had been hidden. When the captain pulled off the sheet of paper, the bomb exploded and blew him to pieces. Four patriots died along with him. Fortunately, it happened early in the morning, so the school was empty. Many of us were grieved by the captain's death. He was the kindest and most respectful of all the policemen on the force. He was just as nice with his subordinates as with everybody here. When he went to people's homes to question them, he was one of the few who knocked politely at the door, greeted everyone, and spoke to them in a mild manner.

Ahmed had a *fatwa* to justify his activities with the GIA.[1] He said, "I'm not the one doing the killing. My hand throws the bomb, but it's not really me. God is the one who is ordering me to do it, and he's the one who guides my hand." When I asked him if it bothered him to see so many innocent people being killed every day as a result of their operations, he replied coldly: "That's war. There are always innocent victims. By paying with their lives, those people are contributing in their own way. Besides, innocent victims who die like that are lucky. They go straight to heaven. They're martyrs."

We saw death daily in Hai Bounab. We lived with it. But to the terrorists, it was all a game. Once, an army helicopter started circling above our heads. The military was stalking some terrorists they had spotted in the orchards. They put in a call to the Eucalyptus brigade to send a patrol to surround our village. The terrorists hid among the trees. Hamid, a neighbor of ours, managed to get them into his house. From there, they went from house to house climbing in and out of the windows until they reached mine and took cover in the underground hideout they'd made. All the while the helicopter was buzzing the village. The police began their search. They went into several homes but not mine. It was built so that you couldn't see the entrance from the street. It was easy to think it was part of the house next door, because the front wall was made of several sheets of corrugated metal lined up end to end. To get in, you had to lift one of the metal sheets, but the police didn't know that. As soon as the military left, Ahmed came out of the hole and told me to get some food ready for them all. They weren't the least perturbed by what had just happened. On the contrary, they thought it was very funny. That's when I realized how egotistical they were, especially my husband. Down there in his underground refuge, he never once stopped to think about me all alone in the yard, trembling with fear. I had stomach cramps from it. The whole time the helicopter was circling overhead—and it circled for over an hour—my biggest fear was that it would bomb the village. If it had, I'd have been the first to get it. I had no way to protect myself. After the incident Ahmed and his friends had lunch and left, as if nothing had happened.

They weren't the only ones to show their self-centeredness that day. My mother-in-law showed hers, too, along with her greediness. She knew I kept some money in the house and came running over the second she heard the helicopter to ask me to give it to her. Seeing how panic-stricken she was, I naively thought she was worried about her son. Well, that wasn't it at all. She came right out and told me that if we were bombed and killed, there was no reason to let the money get blown up too. But I didn't give it to her.

All the people in Hai Bounab knew every one of the terrorists and were perfectly aware of what they were doing. But the villagers were cowards. That's how terror was able to take hold there. They were hostages to the GIA for more than three years. Nobody said a thing the entire time. It was only after those three years that one man dared speak out. That man was Salah, the pharmacist. He had helplessly witnessed a fifteen-year-old boy being tortured, killed, and hacked to pieces just because he was the nephew of a patriot. Salah couldn't stomach what he'd seen and went to tell the police everything he knew the next morning, including the fact that my brothers-in-law were collaborating with the terrorists, giving them food, and lending their cars to them so they could get around. It was following Salah's confession that the patriots killed my brothers-in-law. Salah had to move away under tight military security. They helped him find a place to live somewhere else. And it was a good thing they did because the terrorists came looking for him soon after. They couldn't find him, so they had to make due with burning down his house and everything he'd left behind.

The police, too, were unbelievably lax for a long time. Perhaps they weren't prepared to deal with the terrorist phenomenon. Or were they simply afraid? They were aware of the existence of the armed cells, even though the groups kept a low profile. They knew they were there in the village, that they ate and slept with the people in Hai Bounab. Yet they didn't hunt them down with any real determination. When someone in the area was killed, they made no attempt to find out how it had happened or who might have done it. They just let things slide to the point where the entire population felt that the government authorities had deserted them. Convinced the GIA was in a stronger position, the people sided with the terrorists instead. But when the killings became commonplace, when heads of neighbors rolled in front of their houses, and the school they'd been so proud of was destroyed, they realized they needed to come to their senses. Once they understood what evil the GIA was capable of, they turned against the terrorists and demanded weapons so they could fight back.

16

Death took its toll among the terrorists as well, but they had asked for it. They were playing hide-and-seek with it. As a result, several of my husband's friends died very young. I knew them all. There was Muhammad, for example, Fatma's husband. They nicknamed him "Bouchouour" because of his long hair.[1] And there was Mourad and Djilali. Both were killed in the orchards in a skirmish with the security forces.

Ahmed liked his brothers in the GIA much more than his real brothers. He was especially fond of Rachid. That's why my son's name is Rachid—in honor of him. Ahmed and Rachid did everything together, including joining the guerilla forces in the mountains. My husband was with him the day he was killed. There were three of them: Muhammad, Ahmed, and Rachid. When the military showed up in the orchard, Ahmed managed to climb a tree and stay out of sight. Muhammad fled, camouflaged by the trees. But Rachid was shot in the chest. He fell next to a dried-up well but didn't die immediately. When they saw him lying on the ground, the military took him for dead and left him there to go after Muhammad, who'd escaped. Rachid had compromising documents in the inside pocket of his leather jacket. Although he was dying, he managed to take off his jacket and throw it into the well. Ahmed saw the whole thing from up in the tree where he was hiding but waited until the danger had passed. Unable to catch Muhammad, the military returned for Rachid's body (he actually died two days later at the hospital in Blida). They didn't notice he wasn't wearing his jacket anymore. After they left, Ahmed climbed down from the tree and fished the jacket out of the well. He took the documents and gave the jacket and a watch he found in one of the pockets to Rachid's mother.

Then there was Omar. He lived in Baba Ali and used to come bathe at our house. He was the only one who took the trouble to wash every once in a while. The problem was, we didn't have a bathroom in our house, so I'd clear a spot in the middle of the bedroom and set out a large tub of hot water for him. Naturally, he splashed water everywhere and I had to wipe up after him. Omar died one day in a skirmish in Sidi Moussa. He was twenty-two.

Each time one of them was killed, Ahmed cried endlessly. When I saw him crying over his friends like that, I knew it wasn't just because he was sad. It was also because he envied them for having gone to heaven before him. He wanted to get it over with. He often told me to say a prayer for him asking God to call him to his side while he was in combat. I never did. That's the way all of them said they hoped to die. What they feared most was being arrested and tortured.

Three more of Ahmed's friends were killed at our neighbor Ali's house. Ali had been their staunchest supporter and they had complete trust in him. Nevertheless, he decided to sever all ties with them when they asked if they could dig a hideout at his house, with a tunnel leading to the one under my house—the two houses were separated by three others. What could Ali do? He had to say yes. They started digging, and on the third day Ali invited them to dinner. He had tipped off the police about them, and when Ahmed's friends arrived, the police were there to greet them. The agents had spent two days in the fields across from my house, even sleeping there at night, to observe everyone's comings and goings, yet no one had noticed them. Ali was the only one who knew they were out there. Four brothers were involved, including Muhammad, who was carrying a bag full of money. As soon as they got to Ali's house, the military opened fire. One of the terrorists was killed on the spot. A second was hit in the leg and made his way to my house before collapsing. A third dragged himself to an olive tree, where he died. Muhammad escaped — just as he had before in the orchard. This time he went into a neighbor's house, took three girls hostage, and used them as human shields to keep the soldiers from firing. That's how he got away a second time, carrying the bag of money. The next morning, after the military had left, my mother stepped outside her house and saw Muhammad leaving. He was covered with dirt and still holding the bag of money in his hands. Later that day, the military came back to recover the three bodies. When terrorists are killed in armed conflicts like the one in front of Ali's house, their bodies are taken to the hospital morgue for identification, then the families are notified. The authorities give the parents a document with their son's photo, which they have to bring to the district court. Slain terrorists are always buried by the security forces.

Muhammad miraculously escaped yet another time. He was in Haouch Dubonnet at the home of a woman who lived alone. Ahmed, Fatma, Fatma's husband, and one of their friends were there, too. Someone had tipped off the authorities about them. As soon as the police surrounded the house, the three terrorists somehow sneaked into the house next door without being seen. The woman there told them to hide under the three small beds in the living room. Then she pulled the bedspreads down so that they hung to the floor. When the military came in, they didn't do a thorough search. They usually don't if none of the occupants is a suspect. That was the case in this instance. Next, the military returned to the first house and started questioning the women there. Fatma had pulled her khimar down over her eyes so they wouldn't recognize her, but they knew who she was because of her rings. She always wore one on each finger. One of the policemen remembered that he'd been struck by that detail during an earlier arrest. At the time, he took one of her rings, but she threatened to report him to his superior officer if he tried to take any more from her. On this occasion, the police gave her the thrashing of her life for lying to them and attempting to conceal her identity. She tried to defend herself with yet another lie, accusing her father of having given her over to the terrorists against her will. While the police were beating her, she continued to claim she hadn't seen any of the men they were looking for that day, even though her husband and his two friends were just a few yards away. Meanwhile, Muhammad was able to exit the neighboring house through a back door, disguised in a *hijab*.[2] He was armed, and forced a little boy to walk in front of him to shield him from possible gunfire. The police didn't notice a thing. But they did find items in the garage of the house where the women were: weapons, propaganda, Islamist clothing, and much more. They took it all when they left. They burned down the garage then arrested Fatma and the woman whose house it was. She, too, was beaten at the police station. After two days, they were released.

Muhammad died a few months later. The military fired at him while he was out walking in Hai Bounab. The shots took him by surprise. As he tried to get away, a bullet hit him in the right thigh, but he managed to climb onto the roof of a house and play dead. He had an automatic in his pocket. The military made an unarmed neighbor check to see if he was really dead. As soon as the man approached, Muhammad pulled out his weapon and fired. The police returned fire and hit Muhammad in the chest. As he was gasping his last breath, he cried out for his mother. He was probably sorry for having caused her so much pain. She had walked out on him in a rage three months earlier. She used to live in her own house in Haouch Gros, near Boufarik. The patriots had killed her husband, who was also a terrorist. Fearing they might kill his brothers as well, Muhammad asked his mother to come live with him along with all her other children. Every time her son changed locations and moved to a different house—each one paid for by the GIA—she went, too. The last place was Douar Lahdjar. She stayed there until the day the terrorists decided to smash her TV. Muhammad was breaking everybody's TVs at that point, so he couldn't very well spare his mother's. His brothers wouldn't have approved. Muhammad's mother didn't see it the same way. "It's your fault my eight children can't go to school," she told the terrorists. "And with this cold, they have to stay indoors. They're bored. Let them at least have the television to keep them occupied." They wouldn't listen to her, so when Muhammad was out one day she left with her other children. She came back a week later, though, to pick up the wages the GIA regularly doled out. Muhammad was bitterly disappointed in her. He decided that, as far as he was concerned, she wasn't his mother anymore. The day he died, he regretted his reaction.

17

Ahmed was promoted to the rank of emir at exactly the wrong time. The tide was beginning to turn, and people weren't backing the GIA anymore. In fact, it was becoming increasingly common for them to rebel against its dictates and even fight the militants off with weapons. The easy period the organization had experienced over the previous two or three years was definitely over. But just as no one could have predicted how quickly the terrorist phenomenon would spread, no one expected it to fall apart so fast. The turning point for Ahmed and me was the day of the presidential elections. It marked a new era for us—a time of fear, of being hunted down and always on the run. It was humiliating, especially for me, because I was the one who had to deal with the police every day.

In the middle of the afternoon on election day, my brother-in-law, Bilal, came bursting in. He was pale and out of breath as he gave Ahmed the news: "The police nabbed Nouredine (my other brother-in-law). He's at the police station. They're beating the life out of him right now. They're looking for you. And your wife, too." Ahmed turned to me: "This time it's serious. You've got to leave. Don't stay in the house. You can be sure they'll come here. I don't want them to find you. Go to my uncles' in Benramdane." I was starting to get my things together when he said, "Make us lunch before you go." Neither he nor his brothers seemed in any rush to go into hiding. That's how they were. They always wanted to see danger close up. I was the one who was terrified. As for them, they had a leisurely meal. After they finished, Bilal drove me to Benramdane. His uncles were surprised because they weren't expecting us. They wanted to know what was going on, and I told them. I blurted out the whole story without skipping a single detail. That really annoyed Bilal. He kept winking at me to get me to shut up. He knew they'd be frightened and refuse to let me stay with them. But I went on anyway because I didn't want to deceive the very people I was asking to give me shelter. And, naturally, what Bilal had been afraid would happen did. The only thing Ahmed's uncles could focus on was the prospect of the police showing up one day to look for me. And what would the neighbors think then? Bilal had to get his mother to persuade them that there was absolutely no risk involved for them and it would just be for a few days. After she pleaded with her brothers, practically on her knees, they finally gave in. But they made me promise I wouldn't overextend my welcome and would only stay a few days. In reality, compassion was less of a motivating factor in changing their minds than my mother-in-law's couched insinuations that, if they refused, Ahmed's wrath would be beyond belief. The three uncles lived in adjoining houses. They had long been aware of their nephew's strong ties to the GIA. Their wives told me they'd already had to hide Ahmed on a few occasions when the police were conducting routine searches. He wasn't on the wanted list back then, but all the patriots in Benramdane knew who he was and what he was doing. If you want to avoid trouble with the security forces, it's better not to have anyone who isn't a member of the household present when they come by—nothing that might arouse suspicion. All the villagers in the Mitidja region know that.

I spent a week with Ahmed's uncles. When Ahmed finally resurfaced, they were happy at first because it meant they would be relieved of the heavy burden he had placed on them. They pleaded with Ahmed to take me with him. Not surprisingly, that didn't suit his purposes. Actually, his intention in coming was to convince them to keep me for a few more days. But he didn't want to provoke them. He was afraid they might turn him in. The lack of trust between them was reciprocal. After thinking it over, he decided it would be safer for me in Hai Bounab. Everyone in the village knew and feared him. He was like a cat on its own turf there. But he needed to find me a hiding place. I couldn't very well go back home or stay with my parents. So he took me to Ali's house.

Ali worked in a furniture factory in Algiers and was Ahmed's friend. He wasn't a member of the GIA but supported it fully. Consequently, the GIA was very generous to him. The terrorists gave him money at the end of each month and helped him buy construction materials to enlarge his house—although he still hadn't gotten around to doing it. One room and a kitchen was all he had, but he welcomed me very graciously. I was a friend of his daughters. They made up a bed for me in the kitchen where they and their mother usually slept. Ali and his sons slept in the other room. One of his daughters, Karima, was my age. The day after I got there, Ali sent her to Medea so he could pass me off as her. "You're one of my daughters now," he told me. "If the police come, all you have to do is say you're Karima." After that, everyone in the family started calling me Karima, and I quickly got used to my new name.

Regardless of the tight situation we were in, Ahmed didn't change his routine in the least. He realized we weren't in our own house and he knew I was weak because I was in my first month of pregnancy, but he wouldn't leave me in peace. He insisted I continue with the chores I'd been doing before, namely, cooking for the group. Ali's wife, Khadidja, was already dealing with her own family of ten. Nevertheless, when she saw me sweating away at the stove, she felt obliged to give me a hand. Her intentions were good, but she wasn't much help because her culinary skills were limited to country recipes. Ahmed acted as if Ali's house were his own. On occasion, he'd even come spend the night with me—sometimes several nights in a row. When that happened, Ali's entire family had to pile into the kitchen so Ahmed and

I could sleep together in the only other room in the house. Sometimes he just spent a few hours with me and left in the middle of the night. Everyone stayed up waiting for him to go. I was at Ali's one month.

Passing me off as Karima was a great tactic. It worked really well. Once, in the beginning, the patriots thought they had noticed some unusual activity in the house and came to inspect the premises. It was early in the morning and everyone was still asleep. They surrounded the house and came in. When they questioned Ali, he remained calm, showed them the family record book, and said: "She's my daughter, Karima." The patriots fell for it.

On another occasion I was having breakfast (all I ate in the morning when I was pregnant was some lemon, and, as luck would have it, there was a lemon tree in Ali's yard). The patriots came storming in. One of them yelled at Khadidja: "Get your sons out here. They're terrorists and we know it." She retorted that none of her sons were terrorists. "Yes, but we know you help them," they fired back. Without showing the slightest emotion, she challenged the accusation: "If you have any proof at all of what you're saying, show me." They searched the house from top to bottom but found nothing. While they were questioning her, I remembered something: Ahmed had been by the night before and left his kamis on the bed. I quickly went into the bedroom, took off my dress, slipped the kamis on, and put my dress on over it. Khadidja was fantastic that day. Her responses were as quick and firm as the questions her interrogators shot at her. Even when they were addressing me, she answered to divert their attention. It was intentional on her part because she knew that some of the patriots used to be our neighbors and they might recognize me. But they didn't. The khimar I was wearing down over my eyes covered part of my face, and I had changed a lot during my pregnancy.

The patriots had decided to pay us a visit that day because, the night before, a fifteen-year-old boy who was the nephew of one of the men had been murdered. His throat had been slit, his body chopped to pieces and thrown into a ravine. The patriots found out Ahmed and his group were responsible. They had done it after Ahmed had stopped by Ali's. It was Salah, the pharmacist, who had informed the patriots. When they didn't find anything suspicious at Ali's house, they went directly to my mother-in-law's and ordered her two sons to follow them. They also rounded up my father as well as Kamel and Rafik, two other young neighbors whose brothers were terrorists. They made them all walk to the spot where the boy had been killed and right then and there they executed my two brothers-in-law along with Kamel and Rafik. Kamel was by far the nicest boy in the village. He wasn't known to be a GIA activist, but he may have helped his brothers secretly. As for Rafik, he was only fifteen, like the boy who was killed the night before. Their bodies were tossed into the same ravine where the remains of the patriot's nephew had been thrown. Realizing Ahmed would get wind of what happened, the patriots warned everyone in the village: "You've murdered one of our people. We killed four of yours. If you so much as touch one more of ours, we'll kill all the men in the village." The only reason my father's life was spared was because Salah interceded, explaining that my father had nothing to do with the terrorists. And it was true, he was of no interest to the members of the GIA because he had nothing—no money to give them, no car to loan them, no store where they could get supplies. He had given them his daughter—that was more than enough.

That day, Ali almost died of fright. Khadidja proved to be more courageous than her husband. He kept circling like a lion in a cage and repeating: "They're going to kill us all." Once he got hold of himself, he went to get news from the villagers. He came back half an hour later and announced: "They just killed your two brothers-in-law. You've got to leave. You'll have to find somewhere else to live. I can't let you stay here any longer. Sooner or later they'll end up finding you and my whole family will pay because of it."

I have to admit that only the death of my oldest brother-in-law saddened me. I cried for him because he'd been very kind to me. He was the only one in my husband's family who treated me with any consideration.

18

Khadidja agreed with Ali that I should leave. I didn't know where to go. I didn't have an ID, and with all the police swarming around, I was afraid to be out alone without one. I tried explaining that to Khadidja: "I don't want to cause you any trouble, but if you want me to leave, come along with me. The police will think you're my mother." She said she would if I promised not to come back. She put on her hijab and dragged her two little girls with us. The four of us went outside only to come face to face with the police and the patriots in the street. There was no one else around. I was wearing my *niqab*.[1] The patriots looked it over carefully, trying to figure out whose face was concealed behind it. "Where are you headed?" one of them grunted at me. I thought I was going to collapse on the spot. Khadidja sensed that I felt faint and took hold of my arm to brace me. No sound came out of my mouth. I was afraid my voice would tremble and give me away. Once again, Khadidja showed her courage and answered for me: "This is my daughter, Karima. I'm taking her to the hospital." The patriot hesitated a moment. "Are you sure she's your daughter?" he asked pointedly. She handed him the family record book that she had had the presence of mind to take with her before leaving the house. Once he saw that the name Karima was indeed listed there, he handed it back to her apologetically and let us go on our way. At last I could breathe again.

Khadidja had no idea where to take me. She brought me to her relatives in Eucalyptus, thinking they might be able to put me up for a few days. When we got to their house, they were surprised to see her with a stranger. Before, people used to open their doors to everyone. But now, with what was going on, they had become extremely distrustful. Khadidja introduced me as one of her husband's cousins from Medea. Before she had time to explain the reason for our unexpected visit, a man came in, shouting excitedly: "The patriots are hunting down a woman and her husband. They want to kill them. They haven't found them yet, so they killed the husband's brothers instead." Then after a moment's silence, he added: "You should see those boys' mother. She's gone crazy. She's wandering around screaming in the streets." I thought the man had recognized me. I got a tight feeling in my chest and felt sweat breaking out all over my body. I told Khadidja under my breath that I wanted to leave immediately. "There'd be nothing worse to arouse suspicion," she replied. "Let's wait a bit." Pretending to be only vaguely interested in what the man had said, we sat and had coffee. I had a hard time getting it down. Then we bid our hosts goodbye. It wasn't the best day to be looking for a place to hide. Everyone was suspicious of everyone else.

We had to head back to Hai Bounab. On the way, I saw my mother-in-law in the distance. She never took off her headscarf, but that day she was bareheaded and walking along the blood-spattered dirt trail. Every so often she'd stop, drop to the ground, and roll back and forth. Her white dress was stained red and brown. She was making sweeping gestures with her arms. It was obvious she didn't know what she was doing. She'd go up to her sons' bodies lying in a pool of blood, wrap her arms around them, and sob, then get up and start walking every which way, shrieking like a wild animal. My heart sank as I watched her carrying on like that. I felt a great sadness come over me. I had barely taken a step in her direction to go console her when Khadidja pulled me by the arm. "No!" she said sternly. She knew how much my mother-in-law hated me and was certain that, in her hysteria, she'd accuse me of being responsible for the death of her two favorite sons. "If she sees you, she'll run straight to the police," Khadidja told me. So I had to restrain myself. My mother-in-law kept going back and forth between her house and the place where her sons' bodies had been thrown—a distance of several hundred yards. She kept making the same movements and letting out the same heartrending cries. Every once in a while she'd sing the chant for the dead, the one professional mourners used to sing long ago. It was unbearable. Seeing so much grief, I couldn't hold back the tears. No one made any attempt to go to her. The neighbors watched her, isolated in her growing madness. No one said anything or tried to help her. After the horrific scene had gone on for about an hour, a woman who had also lost two sons a few months earlier found the courage to go to her and, with a great deal of patience, was able to persuade her to return home.

Khadidja took me in again without hesitating for a second. She was so upset by what we'd just witnessed that she didn't have the heart to send me off alone to the fate awaiting me. As soon as we got there, her daughters gave us the news: their father had suffered a heart attack and had been taken to the hospital. It was Friday, the day of rest. To quell his fears, he'd gone to the mosque in Baraki to pray but collapsed after the service. Khadidja looked at me accusingly although she didn't say anything. I think she must have been exhausted.

When Ali was released from the hospital the next day, he made it clear to me that there was no way I could stay at his house. "I don't want to die, me and my whole family, because of what you've done," he told me. My apprehension at the thought of having to set out again to find a place to hide gave me the courage to stand up to him and say things I'd never have dared tell him before: "When my husband was important, you were happy to welcome me into your home. Now that the tides have turned, you've changed sides, too!" What I said really struck a chord, but it ultimately hardened his resolve. I had no alternative but to leave.

Not knowing where else to go, I knocked at my parents' door. My father answered. The minute he saw me, he slammed the door in my face without saying a word. I realized at that moment I was hopelessly alone. It was futile to try to find a Good Samaritan to help me. No one would give me shelter that night. Since I had nothing more to lose, I tried something crazy: I went to my mother-in-law's. She had calmed down somewhat thanks to the neighbor, who had managed to find the words to console her. But as soon as I appeared on her doorstep, she became just as hysterical as before—screaming, insulting me, and calling me a murderer: "Get out of here. I don't know you. You aren't my daughter-in-law anymore. You're the one who killed my sons." She was shouting loud enough for the whole village to hear. It was too much. The world was falling apart all around me. What could I do? I broke down in tears. I understood her pain and only wanted her to understand mine. I tried to win her over: "How can you accuse me of such a thing? Can't you see the predicament I'm in? I don't even have a place to sleep tonight." She was incapable of listening. I asked her to at least give me my family record book. She refused. "It belongs to my son, not to you." There was no point insisting.

I left and wandered aimlessly through the streets, crying. When the neighbors saw me coming, they shut their doors and windows, afraid I'd ask for shelter—the same neighbors who not so long before had treated me like a princess. It was getting late, night was beginning to fall, and I was stuck outside alone. I went back to Ali's and pleaded with him to help me find a solution. He refused again. Seeing me roaming like a lost soul, my mother took pity on me. She went to see Kamel's and Rafik's father. His sons' funeral was going on at the time. She asked him to let me spend the night there. He agreed but told my mother it was only because there were a lot of people at the house that night and no one would notice. I'd have to be out by morning.

I spent three nights at his house. I'd leave early each morning and just walk around the village. When I couldn't go on anymore, I'd walk to what used to be my house. The patriots had torched it the day after I went into hiding. Some of the neighbors gave me food: bread or a tomato. . . . I ate whatever they offered me, waiting for nightfall in the burned-out house. My mother sent my little sister to keep me company because she knew I was all alone and bored in that cold dark house. It was winter, a few days before Ramadan, 1996. I had nothing to use to cover myself. I found a small plastic jerry can in the yard and used it as a pillow. I lay down on a burlap bag I had once used as a doormat. Fortunately, being pregnant made me need a lot of sleep, so, despite the cold and the hard floor, I was able to catch up on the rest I'd been deprived of. It helped take my mind off the time. At least a bit. I had caught lice from sleeping anywhere and everywhere. When I was awake, my sister would pick them off me. Every evening, once the sun began to set, she started to cry at the thought of leaving me alone in total darkness. She always had to be the first to leave because we didn't want the neighbors to see her with me and find out I was in my house. I didn't even light a candle because I was afraid someone might notice. Then, when it was completely dark, I'd go knock on the door of Kamel's and Rafik's parents. They were amazed at how brave I was. But I had reached a point where I couldn't feel anything anymore, much less fear the dark.

On the fourth day, Kamel's and Rafik's funeral ended and the relatives all left. Their father told me I had taken advantage of his hospitality. That night I was once again faced with the problem of finding a place to sleep. I spent the day hiding in my house, as I'd done up till then, but when evening came I went to Ali's and boldly threatened him: "If you don't let me stay with you, I'll tell the police everything." "If you turn me in, you'll get it too," he retorted. I think I really would have gone to the police. In my situation, I had nothing more to lose. If it was a choice between sleeping outside or in prison, I preferred prison. Ali could see how determined I was, so he gave in.

19

By coincidence, Ahmed showed up at Ali's that same night. I hadn't heard from him in a week. I broke down and cried the minute I saw him. I couldn't contain my anger and started swearing at him. It was the first time I had ever dared talk to him that way. I suddenly vented all the resentment that had been building up over the past months. "You claim to be fighting to defend people's rights, but you've left me, your own wife, without shelter to drift from house to house." Then I let fly the supreme insult for someone as macho as he was: "You're not a man!" That got him at the core. What bothered him most was that other people were there to witness the argument. According to Islamist thinking, a wife is never supposed to raise her voice to a man, especially her husband. He was seething but tried to calm me down and get me to stop. He needed to save face: "Everyone here treats me with deference and respect, but you're humiliating me in public." That just upset me more, and I started yelling even louder, so he changed his tactic. He was infuriated: "If you don't shut up right now, I'll kill you." He was loading his mahchoucha as he threatened me. Seeing the gun pointed at me was like getting hit with a club. I knew he could have easily pulled the trigger. I stopped yelling, and the tension eased a little. He thought for a minute, then made a proposition: "If my mother agrees to take you in, I'll buy her a house in another village not far from here and the two of you can live together." I asked why he didn't just buy me the house so I could finally have a place of my own where no one could kick me out, but he categorically refused: "I don't want you staying by yourself. What will people say when they see my wife living alone?" The truth is, he didn't really trust me. He thought a young woman alone was subject to all kinds of temptations. And if he was gone too long, some patriot or policeman could trick me into turning on him.

I wasn't thrilled at the prospect of living with his mother, but I had to accept his offer. What counted most for me at that point was not having to wander around constantly or be subjected to verbal abuse. I was willing to put up with my mother-in-law's goading remarks in exchange for some stability in my life. Ahmed decided the best thing would be to get a little place near my paternal uncles in Cheraga. That way they could keep an eye on me. It was a relief to think I'd finally be able to settle down somewhere. I even started smiling again. That was the first night in a long time that I was able to sleep without having nightmares. I woke up at sunrise. Ali and I went to Cheraga first thing in the morning to ask one of my uncles to look for a house in his neighborhood for us. There were a fair number of houses being built in the area. Owners often rented or sold them cheaply before finishing them.

I was excited. But I didn't even get the chance to knock at the door of my youngest uncle, because when my other two uncles saw Ali and me coming, they went into an uncontrollable fit of rage. They'd heard I was wanted by the police and, since they didn't know Ali, they assumed he was one of my husband's terrorist friends. They didn't want to get even remotely involved in my business. Without so much as listening to what we had to say, they chased us away like thieves and threatened to call the police. They even forbade Ali from ever setting foot anywhere near there again.

We were ashamed. We looked like two dogs with their tails between their legs as we retraced our steps to Ali's house. I spent yet another night there. The next morning, Ahmed took me to a farm in Ouled Allel. I stayed there a week with the widow of another terrorist, her children, and her mother-in-law. After her husband and father-in-law had been killed in Haouch Gros, the two women decided to move to Ouled Allel so they could be among friends. Security forces had never set foot in the village. Hadda joined me a few days later. Each night, our husbands came and slept there as well. We women spent all day every day cooking for the armed group in the region. There were a lot more of them than in Hai Bounab. But the house had only a kitchen and three small rooms. It really wasn't big enough to accommodate everybody. Ahmed and I slept in the kitchen along with Hadda and her husband. There were no doors or windows. A sad excuse for a cloth curtain served as a divider, separating our two beds. I told Ahmed the situation couldn't continue much longer.

One day, he came in and announced: "It's all set. I found a place where you'll be safe." He showed me the address. It was in Birtouta, near Boufarik. A family was waiting for me there, he said. I made the trip chaperoned by the mother-in-law of the woman I was staying with. The two of us got into a van owned by a private company that had been providing trans-portation service ever since terrorists along the bus routes had torched most of the public buses. But just as we reached Birtouta and were getting out of the van, the woman accompanying me noticed an army roadblock. Military personnel were searching the passengers of another van. We weren't carrying anything suspect, but she was afraid they'd ask me for my ID and she knew I didn't have one. She immediately did an about-face and left me there. All she had to say was: "Go on ahead by yourself. You're clever enough. You can manage." After a few seconds, I pulled myself together. I couldn't turn back, too. That would have only made us both look suspicious. So, trying to appear as sure of myself as possible and walking as steadily as I could, I continued on my way. And it worked! No one said a thing to me or even seemed to notice I was there.

I didn't know what the house looked like. All I had were

the directions Ahmed had given me. I discreetly scanned my surroundings until I found the brown door I was looking for. The house looked pretty impressive from the outside. It was obvious that rich people owned it. I knocked. A young man came out, and I gave him the password. It was the name their son used in combat. He was off somewhere taking part in guerilla operations, and nobody except the family knew his code name. The young man showed me in. His mother and sisters joined us. They were delighted to have me as a guest and were very cordial to me. As soon as I was inside and had a chance to look around, I knew the house did indeed belong to wealthy people—the Ghali family from Birtouta. They were well known and respected in the region. The furnishings were just as beautiful and luxurious as the building. Later I found out that the Ghalis owned a tile and construction factory in Sammar, in the industrial sector of Algiers. I was hungry and they served me dinner. Then the lady of the house prepared a hot bath for me in their big, beautiful, all-marble bathroom. It was the most wonderful bath I've ever had. She brought me some clean clothes that belonged to her daughters. Then she asked me the question Islamists always ask: "Do you mind being in the presence of my sons or would you rather not be in their company?" Islamists believe men and women shouldn't gather in the same place. "Now that I'm in your house," I answered, "I consider myself part of your family. I have nothing against being in their company, but I don't want to shake hands with them." She agreed and added: "In any case, that's a sin. We don't do that here either. Women greet men at a distance. That's enough." Madame Ghali had six sons. One was away with the insurgents and another was a member of the GIA in town. Everyone in the family, both male and female, was helping the GIA in his or her own way. They were very devout. The girls always wore hijabs and khimars and prayed constantly. They spent their evenings reading the Koran. The sons took care of family matters and worked for the cause from morning till night. They were happy to meet me and asked all sorts of questions about what things were like in Hai Bounab and the vicinity because their zone of operation was around Birtouta.

The next afternoon Madame Ghali gave me some new clothes she'd just bought in Boufarik. It was the first day of Ramadan and my first day of rest in weeks. When it came time to break the fast, the whole family gathered around the table. We had barely taken the first bite when Madame Ghali began to cry. She was remembering her son, off fighting somewhere, and her daughter, who had just married. Since Madame Ghali had so many children, her house had always been full. But now she felt it was emptying all too quickly. She was thinking about her other two sons as well. They were risking their lives daily. She stopped eating. The atmosphere was pretty gloomy for the first day of Ramadan. Luckily, just as we were finishing, Ahmed and one of Madame Ghali's terrorist sons barged into the living room. The mood changed immediately. She was elated. She set the table again for the newly arrived guests and ate with them. She had regained her appetite. Ahmed spent a few hours with me. The house was so big, we could seclude ourselves in a bedroom without bothering anyone. Then he left and I didn't see him for two weeks—until he sent for me to take me somewhere else.

Unfortunately, I only got to stay with the Ghalis two weeks. I say "unfortunately" because those were the most peaceful and relaxing days I had spent since knowing Ahmed. It was the only time in my married life I was able to sleep as long as I wanted, in a comfortable bed, in a house with heat. And above all, I didn't have to slave away like a workhorse. Madame Ghali treated me nicely and wouldn't let me help her daughters with the housework. In any case, she had two cleaning ladies. Just like a mother, she'd always tell me: "Take it easy so your baby will be healthy." The Ghali boys were very kind to me. They brought me presents every day. I was embarrassed to accept them. That was the first time I was around men my family didn't know. It was so new to me that I began entertaining thoughts not appropriate for a married woman and even dreamed about them. During my two-week stay there, I noticed that a lot of terrorists stopped by the house, especially at night and in groups. They ate dinner there, held meetings, and so forth. The family had many guests. Wives of other terrorists came to see Madame Ghali regularly, and vice versa. The women had established a close network. Their visits gave them the opportunity to find out each other's needs and respond to them. It was their way of being politically active.

The Ghalis aren't the only wealthy family that helped the GIA. I know of another man, Azzedine, who also lives in Birtouta. He had a chocolate and cookie factory but quit his business to join the insurgents.

20

After I'd spent two weeks living in a dream too good to be true, a man brought me a message from Ahmed. I had never seen the man before. He came by car with his two little girls. When terrorists and their friends go anywhere, they usually take children along so they'll blend in with the crowd better. All the man told me was that I was supposed to go with him. I followed his orders. The whole time we were in the car, he didn't say a word. I tried asking him questions, but he wouldn't even tell me where we were headed. After a long ride—and numerous detours—I recognized the road leading to Hai Bounab. The man dropped me off at my parents' house then drove away without saying a thing. To this day, I have no idea who he was. Ahmed arrived a few minutes later and immediately started chewing me out. I had written him a letter a few days earlier and slipped it to one of the Ghali boys. He demanded to know how I could have dared to do such a thing. I just wanted to find out how he was. Naturally, he never answered my letter. His only comment was: "You've shamed me in front of my friends. Their wives don't send them letters!" Once his anger had subsided, he said he'd found a house for me. What a relief! It made me forget the unfair ordeal he'd just put me through. I was in seventh heaven. The reason Ahmed didn't want me staying with the Ghalis was that he felt uncomfortable around them. He couldn't act the same way he did with the people in Hai Bounab. And he wanted the reassurance of knowing I wasn't too far away.

The house he found for me belonged to Khalti Zohra, an elderly woman who'd been living alone in Hai Bounab ever since her sons had moved to Chlef to get away from the terrorism.[1] She had refused to abandon her home and go with them. Ahmed and his brothers took advantage of the fact that she was out that day. They forced the door open and had Fatma and me settle in. Khalti Zohra couldn't believe it when she got back that evening. She was both surprised and afraid. Fatma and I did our best to reassure her, but she didn't want to listen. She was petrified that the terrorists might kill her and take her house. A little later, when Ahmed came back with his friends, he politely asked her to stay and keep an eye on us: "They're both young women. We don't dare leave them by themselves. It would be nice if you could keep them company. Like a mother." Under the pressure of the moment, she consented. But first thing the following morning, she got a truck, loaded it with her meager possessions, and went to her daughter's house in Haouch Pastel. She made sure to take everything, including an old blanket I had brought from my mother's. Fatma and I were left there with nothing but the cement floor—and it was freezing. I was shivering and losing blood. Fatma had her daughter with her. She was only three months old. I combed the house for something we could use to protect ourselves from the cold, but there was nothing. All Khalti Zohra had left behind was an old broken derbouka thrown in a corner.[2] I flipped it over and sat on it so I wouldn't be in direct contact with the icy cement. When our husbands came back that evening to ask how things were going, they saw that the house was completely empty. They were no help. All they did was tell us to stick it out until the next day. Then they left, claiming they had "important things to do."

On their way to wherever it was they were going, Ahmed and Muhammad swung around to Haouch Pastel. They knew the only place Khalti Zohra could be was at her daughter's. They threatened to kill her and take her house permanently if she didn't go back to chaperone us. Their fear was that if the patriots or police found out we were alone, they'd make trouble for us.

When Khalti Zohra returned the next day, she found us both chilled to the bone—especially Fatma, who'd taken off her hijab and used it to bundle up her baby. Around one in the afternoon, Ahmed and Muhammad showed up with a truckload of goods. There was enough to fill an entire house: furniture, a stove, blankets, and dishes. Nothing but expensive foreign brands, and everything was new. There was even a washing machine, which I never used because I didn't know how it worked. Besides, the laundry they gave me was so filthy that a washing machine couldn't have gotten it clean. In addition to everything else, there were two large baskets laden with provisions. All the goods had been taken from the homes of two patriots they'd killed the night before. That's why they'd said they had things to do. It was common for terrorists to clean out the houses of the people they murdered or of emigrants who were away. "It's the spoils of war. It belongs to us," they explained. That day's booty included new clothes for Fatma and me. But Ahmed had no taste. I never liked the clothes he got me.

We spent two weeks at Khalti Zohra's house and felt right at home. In fact, we even had a wedding for one of Ahmed's friends there. The group gave the bride all the household furnishings she would ever need—even a radiator and a fan. Khalti Zohra was with us constantly. We had become friends. Since she knew how to sew, she made a few things for Fatma, the baby, and me. One day she told me she needed some sewing supplies, and we went to Baraki together to get them. Our husbands had ordered us not to let her go out alone. They were suspicious of everyone. On the way back, just before we got to the house, Khalti Zohra said, "It's not far. How about if you go on without me? I need to stop by the Eucalyptus town hall to pick up my monthly pension." I trusted her and did as she suggested. By nightfall she still hadn't returned. Ahmed and his friends were there and knew something was wrong. After she left me Khalti Zohra had gone to the police and told them the whole story.

She even embellished it a bit. Two days later we were surprised by gunshots at dawn. A member of the group was on watch outside as usual. He was the one who had fired the shots, to alert us. The police were surrounding the house. They had kept tabs on our every move over the past two days before attacking.

The military charged in. Once the initial shock and confusion had passed, I was overwhelmed by a tremendous sensation of relief. I think I had the same sensation when I gave birth—a feeling of deliverance after all the pain that had been tearing at me from inside. As they were hauling us to the police station, I was overtaken by a profound weariness. It grew stronger the further we got from the house, and was strangely pleasant. It was a combination of anxiety and release. For once, my fate didn't depend on me. I could chalk it up to destiny. Nevertheless, I tried to resist. For the sake of appearances. And probably out of pride. I mouthed off to the police to show them I wasn't afraid and would not be pushed around. As I watched them, I have to admit I had mixed feelings deep down. Feelings of hatred and anger for sure, but feelings of thankfulness as well. Yes, I was grateful. Grateful to them first of all because they were freeing me at a time when, especially because of my pregnancy, I didn't know if I'd ever see the light at the end of the tunnel. And above all I was grateful to Khalti Zohra. She didn't even realize it, but by turning us over to the police she had gotten me out of the trap I'd been caught in. It was as if the chains that had bound me for so many years had finally been broken. I never saw Khalti Zohra again. She'll probably never know the immense favor she did for me.

21

That military operation took place in late March 1996 and was conducted by combined forces: police, military, and self-defense groups. They arrived at around six in the morning in several vehicles and surrounded the house. Ahmed was there with eight of his friends. Fatma was sleeping with her husband in one of the bedrooms. I had already been up for a while, getting breakfast as usual. Ahmed was awake too. As soon as we heard the first shots, we knew someone had informed the police. Ahmed and his friends were gone in a flash. Most of the houses in the village are right next to each other and aren't built on raised foundations. It's easy to escape by jumping from one window to the next. Naturally, the neighbors were panic-stricken and too afraid for their own lives to yell out or do anything to stop them. Besides, they were more scared of the terrorists than of the police. The orchards encircle the village. Once you made it to that point, there was no better protection than the trees. The terrorists knew where each one was by heart. In his haste, Ahmed forgot his gun on the nightstand. I called him back to get it. When he left, he said, "Take care of the money." I was deeply offended. Here he was leaving me to face the military and the police on my own and he didn't have a single word of concern for me. All he could think about was the money.

The military stormed into the house. There were six or seven men. I can't remember exactly. The others stood guard outside. Fatma broke down as soon as she saw them. She was mostly worried about her daughter. The officer was visibly annoyed by her crying. He chose to ignore her and addressed me instead. I probably looked more composed.

"Where are they?" he asked.

"Who? There's nobody here but us," I replied.

Not surprisingly, the officer didn't believe me, but he realized they had come too late. They had just missed nailing nearly the entire Hai Bounab terrorist cell.

I don't know what came over me, but I had an irresistible urge to throw the police off track. It's true I wanted it to be over and done, but at the same time, I refused to make the job any easier for those taghout my husband was fighting so relentlessly. After all, I was fighting them, too. I have no idea if it was the best thing to do, but I felt I had a role to play, and it was my duty to play it. It would have been too easy to simply admit to everything up front. The soldiers checked all the rooms. They looked around but didn't really do a search, so they didn't find anything of interest at first. They went outside only to come back a few minutes later with a man who'd remained in the yard at a distance. He was wearing civilian clothes, and a hood covered his face. He, too, had informed the police about us. He was a neighbor and knew us all. There must have been gaps or inconsistencies in the information Khalti Zohra had supplied, otherwise the military wouldn't have had to resort to getting a second witness.

Pointing to Fatma and me, the officer said, "Take a good look at these women. Are they the ones you know?"

"Yes, they are," the hooded man replied.

His voice was familiar, but I couldn't place it. I found out much later that he was a young man who had collaborated with the GIA a few months earlier. After his comrades-in-arms killed his brother, he turned against the group and asked for "penitent status" so he could fall under the protection of the *rahma* law.[1] The police did another search. This time it was much more thorough. They found a small cloth bag full of money—sixty thousand dinars—under a bunch of clothes in the closet. They took it, along with some other items and accessories that members of the group used for their rituals: siwak, henna, musk (which they drink before an operation to slow down bleeding if they're wounded), several copies of the Koran, and Islamist propaganda books. They also found typical GIA terrorist attire.

They discovered a cooking pot, some plates, and dirty silverware in a corner of the yard and deduced that I had served some of the terrorists dinner the night before, which was true. A few of the brothers had eaten outside. The officer asked me where they were. I told him I had no idea.

It was now crystal clear to the military: they were at a GIA terrorist hideout.

"Get out of here, you bitch," shouted a patriot.

Another one came up and asked me if I was married. I don't know why, but I lied once again. I knew it would be in my best interest to cooperate with them, yet that didn't stop me from playing my game of deception. I did it because I was slowly beginning to realize I was living the end of a period of my life—the period I had spent with Ahmed, the emir of the GIA in Hai Bounab. Deep down, I wanted the episode to continue a little longer.

A young military man who'd been silent until then pointed his gun at my stomach and said, "It's no use lying."

I was five months pregnant and it showed, even with the loose-fitting clothes I was wearing. I knew it would be stupid to keep on lying about my personal life, but I still didn't want to give in. I wanted the moment to last as long as possible, so I tried another tactic. It was my way of making a statement in front of all those men in uniform I still considered the emissaries of a heathen government that needed to be overthrown. I had to honor my husband, the emir, and felt it was my solemn duty to do what he would have done. I suddenly started hurling every curse and insult I knew at them. I held nothing back. It wasn't until a patriot went to hit me that I finally stopped. The only reason he didn't strike me was that an officer intervened just in time.

"Take off your khimar," the patriot ordered.

I refused and said confidently, "Since you believe my life is in your hands, just kill me. I'm not afraid of you or anyone else. God is the only one I fear."

"So you're one of them. Admit it! Now we know who you are," the officer roared.

I turned to Fatma and told her bluntly: "Say something. What's the matter with you? Have you lost your tongue?"

She was crying even more uncontrollably. The military ordered us to face the wall. My instincts told me they wouldn't harm us. For some strange reason, I never felt they'd kill us. Except at the end, when I turned to look at Fatma and saw her with her forefinger raised reciting the act of faith out loud, the way people do on their deathbeds. That's when fear and doubt took over. For a fraction of a second, I imagined it was possible. They might slaughter us. Or worse still, torture us. I realized I'd better stop playing around. Then, as if I were under a spell, all my muscles relaxed and I was overcome with great sadness. Before I knew it, I silently began to cry.

22

I truly wanted to be done with the kind of life I'd been living, but I was troubled by the prospect of losing my husband or betraying him—partly because I was afraid he'd do something violent, but also no doubt because I loved him. So, after trying to resist the police, I gave in to despair. Not for long, though. Once the police were sure they'd discovered the Hai Bounab group's hideout, they made Fatma and me go outside. Just then, a man selling bread house to house drove by. The police ordered him to stop. They had Fatma and me get in with him, along with two of the policemen. The rest of them followed us in their cars. As we were getting in, one of the policemen tried to be funny: "You go first. That way if there's a road mine, they'll get it before us." Nobody laughed, not even the other officers. They took us to the Eucalyptus police station (Hai Bounab falls under its jurisdiction). We waited there all day without an inkling as to what was going to happen to us. That evening, a field officer from Blida came to question us.

I regained my cool a bit at the police station and pondered the situation. I thought about Ahmed and my family, my parents and nine brothers and sisters, and the risk I ran of implicating them all in this mess. I wanted to avoid that at all costs. I thought that if I was aggressive with the police, all the blame would fall on me and it would buy time for Ahmed and his friends by allowing them to get as far away as they could. So I went back to playing the game I'd tried in the beginning. I was determined not to show the slightest sign of weakness. And it paid off, because the police treated me with consideration and respect the entire time I was there. When the field officer began interrogating me, I again denied all the allegations except one: that my husband was indeed a terrorist and member of the GIA. But he already knew that. I didn't tell him about all I'd done for the GIA, all the support I'd given the group. It was only after several hours of questioning that I confessed. I even claimed responsibility for things I hadn't done. I was so tired, I just said yes to whatever they asked. My main concern was not to incriminate the neighbors, even though they had played a huge role in allowing the GIA to take root and spread in our village. But was that their fault? Then the officer asked, "Have you ever killed anyone yourself?" That's one question I wasn't expecting. It really caught me off guard. Did he think terrorists' wives were murderers? Noticing my surprise, he deduced the answer on his own. He also asked me if I knew how to handle weapons, and what kind Ahmed and his group used. Naturally I'd learned to load and unload a mahchoucha. But only out of curiosity, nothing more.

The officer called Fatma and me into his office separately for questioning. He treated us politely. The rest of the time, she and I were in the same room. That helped, because we were able to offer each other encouragement—especially now that Fatma had finally stopped crying! Then late that night they transferred us to the station in Baraki. When we got there, they had us remove our belts and jewelry and made me take off my khimar, too, but not my clothes. GIA rumors had it that when the police arrested women, they stripped them naked and left them nude. That didn't happen. They showed Fatma into one of the offices where a cot had been set up. They didn't put her in a cell, because she had her baby daughter with her. They put me in one, though. It was a tiny cubicle with just enough room for a mattress on the floor. There were no openings and there was no light. It was dark and dirty. They brought in a foam mattress covered with bloodstains. The blood was still relatively fresh. It made me want to gag, but I was too exhausted at that point to be finicky. I took off my hijab to use as a sheet and stretched out on it. Images played out in my mind of things I'd seen a few minutes earlier when I went down to the toilets: men, completely naked in a kind of cellar and smeared with blood. I wondered if I could survive such conditions. I didn't want to even imagine the prospect. As it turned out, I was lucky. I wasn't tortured or even slapped around.

I spent three nights in that cell, with no food. Later the police told me they'd forgotten I was there, but I didn't believe them. They wanted to punish me for having stood up to them. On the other hand, Fatma, who did little more than cry, must have gained their sympathy. She acted like she was really sorry for what she'd done. But not me. And besides, I was the leader's wife. My punishment had to be harsher than hers. When a policeman asked me if I still loved my husband, I lashed back with words so sharp they surprised even me: "Of course I do. Aren't there times you want me to love you, too?" That was another reason my punishment had to be harsher. Unlike me, Fatma was allowed to sleep in a clean bed with her daughter, and the police gave her all her meals. They went out and bought powdered baby formula just for her. They also gave her soap to bathe the baby and detergent to wash the baby's diapers. The police enjoyed playing with Fatma's little girl. The only problem was that there was no hot water at the station. The baby had to drink her milk cold and that made her get sick.

The police chief at the Baraki station was very nice. When we were brought in, he asked me my husband's name. He gasped when I told him: "Oh, Chaabani. Your husband tried to kill me. Did you know that? He came all the way to Zeralda. That's where I live." Then, looking at my stomach, he added: "I'm not young anymore, you know." He was in his forties. "I'm still not married and don't have any children. But don't worry. I won't hurt you. I'll let you enjoy the pleasure of bringing your child into the world." He succeeded so well in winning our confidence that Fatma and I felt comfortable with him and told him everything we knew.

The day after I was arrested, I discovered there'd been a massacre in Benramdane during the night. Through the little grate of my cell door, I overheard a conversation in the police chief's office. Someone was sobbing loudly as he told the chief what had happened. The GIA had beheaded eight members of his family. All the heads had been piled into a wheelbarrow and dumped in the middle of the village. I got frightened as I listened—afraid the police would take their vengeance out on me. I started crying. A policeman heard me and yelled in a rage, "So now you decide to cry! See what your friends are doing?"

On the third day they transferred us to the court in Blida and we appeared before a public prosecutor. He happened to be a distant relative of my father's who also lived in Cheraga. He was on good terms with my father and knew me quite well. I'd grown up with his daughters. When he saw me come in, he burst out laughing: "Couldn't you have found a better husband than that thug?" Then he tried to be reassuring: "Don't be scared. I'll take care of you." Next we went before the examining magistrate for questioning. After writing up his report, he sent us back to the police station in Eucalyptus. The captain there summoned my father and ordered him to take us both with him. "Whatever you do," the captain said categorically, "don't let them stay in Hai Bounab. Get your daughter far away. Anywhere but there. And take Fatma to her parents' in Bab Ezzouar." He was concerned, and rightly so, that if we stayed in the village, our husbands would come for us. The only measure the police took against Fatma and me was to put us under surveillance: we had to report to the station every Wednesday.

Even though the treatment we had received was fairly lenient, I was astonished on the third day when the police chief told us we could leave. The fact that he let us go like that showed how inexperienced he was. He never thought we'd go back to the GIA the very next day.

As soon as we were outside the police station, my father told me that about forty terrorists had descended on the house the night before and that they were still there. They'd heard through their informants that he'd been called by the police, and they knew why. The terrorists were waiting for Fatma and me, to take us back with them. And they were holding my brothers hostage. Nevertheless, my father gave us two choices: go somewhere else, like the police chief said, and jeopardize my brothers' lives, or defy the police chief's orders and return to our husbands and their friends. I told my father I trusted his judgment. Actually, I didn't dare say very much because I felt I'd already humiliated him enough. The best thing for me to do was not say anything for once and give him the impression that he still had at least a tiny shred of authority. He thought it over, then said solemnly, "I'm not going to take you back to the house. You can spend the night somewhere else. That way, you'll have time to think it through on your own. You can decide what you want to do tomorrow." He drove us to the home of a very nice lady who lived alone with her daughter, Taous, in Eucalyptus. She put us up for the night.

23

My father arrived early the next morning looking tired, like someone who hadn't slept a wink the whole night. We thought —with some regret, I must say—that he was afraid of the police and was going to do as the police chief had instructed, namely, drive Fatma to Bab Ezzouar and me to one of my aunts outside Hai Bounab. Fatma and I both missed our husbands. When we were all in the car, my father asked me again, "What have you decided?" It was my responsibility to choose because, for one thing, my husband was the leader of the group and, for another, my brothers' lives were in danger. I could see despair and worry written all over my father's face. He hadn't decided anything on his own. He was incapable. It was the first time I'd seen him in such a state. This was a tragedy for him because he was a man who'd never shown courage or determination in his life. Now he had to choose between angering the police or the terrorists. It didn't take him long to decide. He would deal with the wrath of the ones who seemed the least inhumane—the police. Fatma did no soul-searching. What she wanted most was to be with her husband. I have to admit I didn't hesitate for long either. I told my father that, in order to save the lives of my brothers, it would be better for me to go back to Ahmed. I was terrified at the thought that they were being held hostage, but my desire to see Ahmed was certainly a motivating factor in my decision. My father breathed a sigh of relief. "The police will put me in jail and beat me, but the terrorists would slit my wife's and children's throats in front of me," he told us, as if to justify what he was doing.

And, just as he had said, the terrorists were waiting for us at my parents' house. It was a horrible day. My mother gave me some bad news. First of all, she told me a neighbor of ours that I was very fond of had been killed on our account. It happened the day we were arrested at Khalti Zohra's, not long after the police hauled us off. Thinking the police would come back and search her house again, the terrorists had returned and planted a bomb in the bedroom. As fate would have it, Hamid, the redhead, an extremely nice neighbor, came by right afterward. He suspected there might be some money in the house and wanted to be the first to find it. The bomb went off as soon as he opened the door. He was blown to bits. His wife gathered his remains. The scraps of flesh were so scattered that she had to ask neighbors to help her.

My mother had more bad news for me. The explosion had destroyed what little remained of my possessions. Since the room where I had stored everything I owned was right next to Khalti Zohra's bedroom, all my things were now buried under rubble. Earlier, the patriots had burned the other room. I suddenly realized I was homeless. And now Hamid's wife and children were living in poverty with no roof over their heads. When I saw Ahmed a few months later, I asked him if he was the one who'd planted the bomb. He swore to God he wasn't and even claimed the patriots had done it, hoping they could wipe out a couple of terrorists. I believed him, as usual, but Hamid's wife was emphatic: "It was Ahmed, I know it. He and his friends were the last ones there. The patriots never came back after you left." She was certain of it, and others corroborated her account.

The terrorists and our circle of acquaintances welcomed Fatma and me back as if we were queens. As is the custom, the neighbors came to visit and congratulated me on my speedy return to my family and friends. The first question Ahmed asked was if the police had raped us. That's all he could think about. He was sure they had. No matter how I tried to convince him they hadn't, he kept prodding me and used every trick possible to get me to admit that they had. Then he promised he wouldn't hold it against me if I'd been raped, since it had been done against my will. Just to get him to at least pretend he thought I was telling the truth, I had to get angry with him for showing so little confidence in me. But he only half believed me. He stopped asking me questions for a while then got up and said we needed to leave. I told him I couldn't. I was worried about my family because they were under police surveillance. Ahmed never tolerated anything that went counter to his intentions. He didn't take it well when I didn't jump at the chance to go with him. After all, he'd been waiting for me for several days. He said there was only one explanation for my behavior: "OK, I get it. The taghout have won you over. They did something to you, that's for sure. You don't love me anymore." He was out of control and certain he was right. He loaded his mahchoucha and pointed it at my temple: "If that's the case, I'll kill you right here and now." I was trembling with fear. It was hard to get him to understand that I couldn't just ignore the threat looming over the lives of my father and brothers. It was as simple as that. He calmed down but ended up convincing me they weren't in any danger. The group would protect them. So we left my parents' house in the middle of the night and went to Meryem's mother's house in Haouch Dubonnet.

She was the mother of five grown women and three teenage boys and had strong ties to the GIA. She helped the group considerably, giving the members food and logistical support, even though none of her sons were terrorists. Her husband was against it but didn't dare say so. The terrorists nicknamed her "El Fahla (the valiant one) from Larbaa," because that's where she was born. She was a black woman and an excellent cook. I still remember the delicious meal she prepared the night we arrived: stuffed roast rabbit. It was fabulous. She got all her vegetables from her own garden. Her daughters were experts at making pastries and sweets. El Fahla's husband worked on a neighboring farm. They lived fairly comfortably.

When we arrived at their house, El Fahla was engaged in a leisurely conversation with Fatma. She had already prepared dinner and gotten the beds ready for Fatma and me and our husbands. El Fahla's commitment to the cause was boundless. She even built a secret loft just below the roof, where terrorists on the run could hide out. It was practically undetectable and had apparently already been used. El Fahla's daughter told me that a couple of terrorists were dodging helicopter gunfire one day. The first was shot and killed a few yards from the house. The other jumped over the garden wall and landed under the arbor in the middle of their yard. El Fahla's daughter hid him in the loft. He was very handsome, she said. He was injured, so she gave him a rag and some olive oil to tend to his wound. Then she waited for the helicopter to leave before telling him he could come out. It was love at first sight for both of them. He returned a few days later with his friends to ask for her hand in marriage, but she was already engaged to a man from Larbaa and was soon to be married. She still thought about him, and when she spoke of him, her voice was full of admiration, but she knew what she wanted. Despite all the support she gave the terrorists, marrying one was out of the question. That would mean leading a miserable life, like mine. "What you're going through is a lesson for me," she said. The wounded man she'd been attracted to had become a friend of the family and still came by to visit now and then.

I told Ahmed the very first day that I didn't want to stay with El Fahla. The house was too small for so many people. There was her family—ten of them in all—plus Fatma and her little girl, our two husbands, and the terrorists who ate there every day. It didn't really bother Ahmed. What he wanted was to drop me off somewhere, anywhere that was convenient for him. He left me at El Fahla's for the night, but when he came back the next evening I brought the subject up again. "I don't know where you can go," he said. "The only place that comes to mind is Birtouta, with the Ghali family." I jumped at the suggestion. The Ghalis had been so nice to me the last time, and I felt so at home in their big luxurious house. I was happy at the thought of going back there and only hoped I could stay as long as possible this time.

El Fahla and her husband accompanied me to Birtouta. But what a surprise I had when I got there and knocked at the door. Madame Ghali drove me away as if I had the plague. And so did her sons and daughters. "There's no way we're going to put you up again," they yelled in my face. Their house looked totally different. The outside walls had been riddled by gunfire. A few days earlier, there'd been a skirmish between a group of terrorists in the house and the security forces. The police arrested one of the Ghali boys, who was a go-between for the GIA. They didn't get the other son. His parents still had no idea where he was.

There I was out on the street. And strangely, El Fahla and her husband now refused to let me go back with them. I didn't know what to do. Frankly, I was irritated by their reaction. I couldn't figure out why they didn't want me. I didn't even bother to argue with them. I spotted a military roadblock not far away and threatened, in no uncertain terms, to turn El Fahla and her husband in if they didn't change their minds. So they did.

That evening, I had it out with Ahmed: "We're in the way here. Can't you see that? Figure something out. You've got to find a permanent solution. Now." He was in a real bind because he had nothing to propose. "Stay with El Fahla one more night and we'll see what we can do tomorrow," he said. The following evening, he announced he'd solved the problem, and told me to pack. I was so happy at the thought of having a permanent roof over my head that I went with him, even though I didn't know where we were going. It was raining hard that night. In those remote areas, there are no paved roads or streetlights. It takes only a few drops of rain and you're up to your knees in mud. To make matters worse, we decided to cross the fields and take the least traveled path so we wouldn't draw anyone's attention. It was the wrong thing to do. I started bleeding again and was in incredible pain. It hurt so much I was sure I'd lose the baby any minute. Ahmed took my hand to give me support. That wasn't enough. The cramps were tearing my insides apart. I was shivering from the cold and had trouble walking through the mud in the dark. He realized we wouldn't get very far the way we were going, so he decided to carry me on his shoulders, but he couldn't see where he was going either. After about fifteen minutes he put me down to catch his breath. As if things could get any worse, it was so dark that he had unknowingly set me down in a ditch full of water. I was completely drenched. My clothes were soaking wet and were weighing me down. But we had to continue our seemingly endless journey. Finally we arrived at what I thought would be my house. But I was disappointed yet again. We were at Djouher's house, one of Ahmed's relatives who lived with her mother in Haouch Dubonnet. When the two women saw the state I was in, they melted into tears. They gave me clean dry clothes and built a fire to warm me. Djouher had prepared a meal for the whole group. They came for dinner and spent a good part of the evening there.

"I'll be back tomorrow," Ahmed told me as he was leaving. But right after that, he and his friends ran into a police patrol a few blocks away. There was a skirmish and Ahmed was shot in his right arm. I didn't see him for seven months.

24

Muhammad and two friends came by the next day with a message from Ahmed; they said he'd been injured and wouldn't be back for a month. I didn't entirely believe them. I thought Ahmed was more than just hurt. I thought he was dead. Muhammad could see how upset I was and tried to set my mind at ease: "Here's proof he's alive. He told me to drive you to your parents' house if that's what you want. Unless you'd rather stay here." I couldn't stay: Djouher and her mother lived in an old farmhouse way out in the country. It was cold and lacked even the most basic necessities. Trying to communicate with the outside world was a feat in itself. And just by being there I had unknowingly caused problems for Djouher. Her husband left when he found out I'd be spending a few days at his house. He knew I was married to a terrorist and didn't want to have anything to do with them. Djouher was frightened, too, but didn't dare admit it openly. That morning, she said, "If anyone knocks at the door, hide under the bed." Her words only boosted my determination to leave. Frankly, listening to her made me feel like I was in prison.

That's why I had Muhammad take me to my parents. My mother gasped as soon as I walked in. She was sure I'd been killed when I left her house in the middle of the night with Ahmed. She'd heard us arguing and yelling. After we went outside, all she could hear was the brothers praying. As Ahmed and I walked away from the house, they kept repeating, "*Allah akbar, el hamdou lillah*" (God is great, God be praised). It was their way of expressing joy at their victory over the enemy, because the police had released Fatma and me. But my mother thought

Ahmed had killed me after our argument and that the brothers were chanting the prayer for the dead. So when I showed up on her doorstep, she was convinced I was a ghost. She's rather simpleminded, and it took me a long time and a lot of explaining to make her realize I was indeed alive. Fortunately, my father was at work. I'm sure he wouldn't have opened the door to me. "You can stay here under one condition," my mother said. "If you report to the police station this instant." She even helped me come up with an excuse for why I'd missed checking in the week before. We went right away. I explained that I had been at my aunt's in Cheraga and couldn't come to the station because the police had closed off the whole area. It so happened that, on the previous Wednesday, the bomb Ahmed had planted in Khalti Zohra's house went off, killing Hamid the redhead. All the roads in and out of Eucalyptus were blocked.

I spent two days with my parents, despite my father's objections. He did nothing but sulk the whole time I was there. Thinking it over, I decided it would be smarter to leave Hai Bounab because Ahmed could show up at any time and force me to go with him. I was exhausted and having complications with my pregnancy. The prospect of reliving what I'd just gone through terrified me. All I craved was a little peace and quiet. That's when my mother suggested I go to Cheraga and stay with my oldest aunt. She had always been fond of me and would take good care of me. So that's what I did. The following Wednesday when I checked in at the police station, I found out my father had been arrested that morning. Fatma had made accusations against him. They had arrested her two days earlier in Haouch Dubonnet. To get herself off the hook, she put all the blame on my father, accusing him first and foremost of having handed us directly over to the terrorists without asking us what we wanted to do. The police nabbed my father while he was at work at the town hall. I was at the station when my mother burst in looking for him.

I had never seen the Eucalyptus police chief so outraged. When I went into his office, he looked at me with daggers in his eyes. Then he let his anger fly. Until then he hadn't said anything rude to me. But now he was calling me every name in the book. His face was so contorted he could barely breathe as he howled, "You betrayed my trust! You'll pay for this! You're nothing but a dirty slut. Hanging around bloodthirsty terrorists is all you care about. I'm sorry I treated you so decently. But it's not too late, you know. I can still lock you up if I want." I admit that few people get the kind of special treatment he'd shown me up to that point. I hadn't at all expected it. And I knew the situation could change any minute. I sank down into my seat, lowered my eyes, and let him vent his fury. Once he'd gotten it all out, he calmed down. Actually, I think he considered me a victim. Someone who needed help. "I'm giving you one more chance," he said. "But it's the last time. If you level with me, I'll help you get out of the lousy rut you're in." That's when I told him everything, down to the tiniest detail, from the moment I left his office with Fatma and my father right up to that very day. Obviously, I pleaded on my father's behalf, explaining that because of the danger his wife and sons were in he'd had no choice but to comply with the terrorists. My father was released after two days. He hadn't been mistreated, which surprised even him. All the police did was question him. They figured that since he had ties with Ahmed Chaabani and his group, he'd have useful information for them. But they finally had to face the facts: my father knew nothing and never did. He was such a coward that he never showed the slightest interest in what was going on in our village. Whenever a neighbor broached the subject, he'd cut him off and walk away. He was afraid of getting involved. They let Fatma go the same day as my father. This time the police chief made sure to send for her parents to come get her and personally take her home to Bab Ezzouar. Like me, she was supposed to report to the Eucalyptus police station every Wednesday. I informed the captain that I was leaving Hai Bounab and quietly went off to my aunt's.

I have two aunts and two uncles on my father's side living next door to each other in Cheraga. The younger aunt got divorced fifteen years ago and has a sixteen-year-old son. He doesn't know who his father is. Her divorce was a traumatic experience for her. Where we come from, a divorced woman is considered worthless, and her brothers have never let her forget it. She was convinced that if I remained in Cheraga I'd be the cause of yet another divorce, namely, my other aunt's. Nevertheless, that aunt insisted on letting me stay with her. She knew I had no other safe place to go. My younger aunt's apprehensions were well founded. Her sister's husband was against having me in his house. He was afraid it would mean he'd have to deal with the police or the terrorists. My divorced aunt did everything she could to make my life miserable so I'd want to leave, and she succeeded. One afternoon my mother came to visit and accompany me to the town hall to get an ID—my very first. I told her I planned to return to Hai Bounab with her. "But where will you stay?" she asked. She knew my father was still upset with me. "I want to go to Ali's," I said. Ever since Ali had turned Ahmed and his friends in, he and his family had been living in a single room in the building that housed the police station. It was small and filthy. (He later joined the patriots and moved into an abandoned hammam in Eucalyptus.)

And so I spent two nights at the police station—willingly. There were twelve of us crammed into that tiny room. When it rained the ceiling leaked. Worse yet, Ali's family didn't even have the bare essentials. They hadn't had time to take much with them when they fled their house. The police supplied them with a few blankets, but there weren't enough to go around. They were hospitable to me, despite the awkwardness they felt for having tipped off the police about Ahmed. "Don't worry," I reassured them. "I'm free of that life now, too. I have no second thoughts about cooperating with the police."

A week later, the judge gave me permission to live at home. In exchange I promised to help the police capture Ahmed if he showed up. I was willing to do anything to be able to return to my own house and not wander around begging for shelter. But it was too good to be true. Misfortune was still following me. Since Ali was virtually living with the police, he was in constant contact with them. While I was getting ready to go home, he told them about the hideout under the house. As a result, I got another taste of the police chief's anger that day: "You lied to me again. Why didn't you tell me there was a hideout under your house?" I tried to convince him that I didn't know anything about it, that my husband must have dug it when I wasn't around. He seemed to believe my story but told me point-blank, "Since that's the way it is, you can forget about going back there." For a few brief hours, I thought my problem had been solved, but now I was again faced with the question of where to go. I couldn't very well overextend my welcome at Ali's, so I resigned myself to returning to my aunt's in Cheraga.

It was imperative for me to get permanent lodging and decent medical attention. I was growing sicker by the day, and the risk of having a miscarriage was becoming an ever-increasing threat. Despite the dead-end life I was leading, I didn't want to lose my baby. Having the child was crucial. Perhaps because that was all I had left of what was really mine. As I'd anticipated, my aunt took care of me the best she could. After a few days, I was less in danger of having a miscarriage, but I was still weak. Unfortunately, two weeks later, her sister started nagging me again and told me to get out. I talked it over with my mother. She ran through the list in her mind of all the people who might be able to take me in—and the list was getting shorter and shorter. Finally, she remembered two uncles she barely knew on her mother's side who lived in Sammar. She had seen them only on rare occasions, but they agreed to put me up for a few days. I think they were afraid to refuse.

I spent a week with them. In the middle of the week, on my way to report to the police station (that was the only time I got to go out alone), I made a detour to Birtouta to see the Ghali family and ask if they had any news about Ahmed. I hadn't seen him in three months, and his friends had stopped giving me my monthly allowance of three thousand dinars. I had no money, not even enough to pay for my medication, and I still hadn't completely recovered. Although Muhammad dropped by Hai Bounab from time to time to find out how his wife, Fatma, was doing, Ahmed never thought of giving him a cent for me. When I was their official cook, the money came in regularly. Ahmed used to tell me that if he died the monthly payments would continue for the baby and me. It wasn't true. The Ghali family assured me that my husband had only been injured and was being treated in Djouab, near Medea. I was happy to know he was still alive.

25

I had a relapse while I was at my mother's uncles' house. They lived in a remote, underdeveloped area. The lack of hygiene caused me to get an infection. My uncles and their wives were totally indifferent to my condition. I didn't get out of bed for days, yet none of them asked me what was wrong. They couldn't have cared less. I was getting progressively worse and realized nobody there was going to look after me. One evening, when one of my mother's uncles came home, I worked up the courage to talk to him. I told him he had to take me back to my aunt's house in Cheraga—which he gladly did. He was thrilled to get rid of me. Once again, my aunt took care of me until I was better. The following Wednesday, when I reported to the Eucalyptus chief of police, I couldn't contain my desperation. I told him, "I can't go on like this. I'm sick and no one wants to have anything to do with me. I need a permanent place to stay. I want to go home." He granted my request and gave me permission to return to Hai Bounab but not to my house. The police had sealed off the premises because of the hideout. So I went back to my parents', where I stayed for a month, despite my father's recriminations. My mother took care of me for the remainder of my convalescence.

It was June, and the baby was due in August. The smartest plan would be for me to stay at my grandmother's in Zeralda until the delivery. That way I could have my baby in the hospital there. I felt it was the best place to have my baby because no one in Zeralda knew me—not the people, not the police, not even the clerks at the town hall. Besides, I was determined to make sure my son was legally registered like everyone else. The employees at the Eucalyptus town hall could very well have refused, the way they refused to issue me an ID. When the clerk there turned down my application, he made a point of telling me: "We'll give you an ID the day your husband stops burning down our offices." Unfortunately, he was right about Ahmed's activities. But at least he issued me a travel pass. The Eucalyptus police chief was the one who later helped me get my ID.

The baby was born in August at the hospital in Zeralda. Friends who came by all made the same comment: "We thought you'd give birth to a monster, not a human being." Others were actually surprised I was still alive. They remembered how I'd been dragged from one place to another in the dead of winter, and always in the middle of the night or at dawn. My mother was convinced I'd either lose the baby or it would be born abnormal. The worst thing was the mental anguish. Giving birth was an added ordeal. I had never felt so alone and sad before. On the first day, I was hoping someone would come ask how I was doing. No one did—except my elderly, ailing grandmother. Looking at the baby boy I had wanted so badly, I resented him to the point where I refused to breastfeed him, even though my breasts were so heavy with milk it felt as if they were about to burst. There were times I even wanted to hit him. My grandmother brought me to my senses. "He's your son. He needs you. You're all he has," she said. "If you're going to let him starve now, you shouldn't have carried him for nine months."

The doctor taking care of me was a woman. She and the attending nurses spared no effort to get me on my feet again. I didn't have to say a word. They could tell my situation was unusual. I wasn't just another patient. What struck them most was that I'd been left to fend for myself. In our culture it's extremely rare for that to happen to a woman who has just given birth to her first son. They sympathized with me, probably thinking I was an unwed mother: those are the only women who are abandoned the way I was. To make my solitude easier to bear, they brought me presents for the baby. Three days after he was born, my mother came to get me. My grandmother put us up for the night, and we went back to Hai Bounab the next day. My mother couldn't even pay for a cab. My father refused to give her any money because that would be helping "the son of a terrorist." What a great way to start off! So with the baby in my arms and my stitches pulling at me, I got into a Renault J5 that was providing group transportation. My father was waiting for us at the door: "Take your baby and get out of here," he yelled in my face as he blocked the doorway. I was too weak to say anything or even stand up for that matter. I sat down on one of the steps. It was a blessing that my mother was there. When she puts her mind to it, she knows how to get her way with my father. She wasn't about to let him kick me out in the condition I was in. But he warned us both: "No way am I going to pay for any celebrations."

Once again, the neighbors took care of things for me. The first one to come visit was a good friend of mine. Looking at my son, she said, "I hope he won't slit people's throats like his father does." A month later, Ahmed slit her throat. It must have been a premonition. All the women said the same thing: "Let's hope he doesn't turn out like his father." My father finally gave in to my mother's pleas and I was able to stay with them another month—until the day Ahmed came back to make plans to ransack the village.

The day before he arrived, the police were at our house waiting for him. But they were a day too early. The tip they'd received from their informant was accurate, but the group members had decided to put off their return till the following day. The police forced the door open and barged in at around eight at night. And there were a lot of them. They gave the whole family quite a scare. A few minutes after they got there, they made my father go out into the yard. Then we heard gunshots. We thought for sure they had murdered him. The whole family started screaming. The children were yelling, "They've killed Daddy!" My mother was nervously scraping her cheeks with her fingernails and slapping her thighs. But the police had simply fired shots in the air, maybe to let everyone know they were there. As soon as they realized the confusion they'd caused, the squad leader sent my father back in so we could see he was still alive. They must have determined that there was little chance the terrorists would show their faces after all that racket. Or perhaps it was part of their plan. An hour later several of them left to make it look like the danger was over, but five of them stayed. They ate what we had for dinner, and spent the night. Two watched from the bedroom window while the others waited outside. They suggested we turn on the TV to pretend everything was normal. That way, if the terrorists did come, they wouldn't be suspicious. None of us slept a wink. Everyone was on the lookout, for his or her own reason. We were apprehensive of both the terrorists and the police. My little sisters were huddled in a corner and couldn't stop crying. My mother tried to ease my father's nerves. He was scared out of his wits. My brothers were all giving me accusing glances—a reminder that I was the cause of all the trouble. And I was silently praying that Ahmed wouldn't come. I was afraid he'd be killed and that my family and I would get it too. No one dared imagine the bloodbath that would have ensued had the two opposing forces come face to face. And we would have been in the middle. Thank God nothing happened. The next morning the police left empty-handed. That was the only time they spent the night at our house. On another occasion they came rushing in at daybreak thinking they'd find the enemy. That time there were nine policemen in all. They waited around till noon then left. The tip they'd received was wrong. The police and the terrorists were playing a game of hide-and-seek. They often missed each other. Once in a while they'd meet up. Each side had its own spies; sometimes they worked for both groups.

26

After seven months Ahmed came back. In the middle of the night, naturally. Things had turned really ugly throughout the area and the GIA had become increasingly bloodthirsty. The massacres baffled everyone. No one could understand the GIA's cruelty. In the wake of recent events, Ahmed's return was not a good omen. He was with three other terrorists. One came into the house with him while the other two took positions outside to keep watch. He kissed the whole family, except me of course. A man is not supposed to kiss his wife in front of her parents. That's the custom here. He'd changed so much that I mistook him for someone else at first. I'd never seen him with a beard before. It hung all the way down to his chest. He used to hate them and could only stand a moustache if it was small and closely trimmed. He was wearing a black headscarf and Afghani clothes that were so filthy I couldn't even make out the color. The brown jacket he had on over them was just as dirty. Initially I didn't notice that his arm was wounded. When he took off his jacket, I saw he had a well-stocked leather cartridge belt crisscrossing his chest, and his arm was bandaged. He could move it slowly but didn't have enough use of it to do any real work. A heavy atmosphere suddenly descended over the household. We were all expecting him to make some sensational announcement or order us to do something insane. We all knew his visit had a purpose.

Then, for once, my father stood up to Ahmed and lambasted him: "How could you leave your wife and not contact her for seven months when you knew she was pregnant?" My father told him I'd been very ill and that it was a miracle I'd given birth with only minor complications. Ahmed said nothing. He had no answer. Then he and I went into the bedroom, just the two of us. That's when he told me in a tone bordering on helplessness, "I didn't forget about you. I asked my uncle to bring you a message to let you know I was badly injured and would be back as soon as I could." His uncle never gave me the message. He knew I had to report to the police station every week, and he was probably afraid I'd tell the police. Then they'd go interrogate him to find out when and where he'd seen his nephew. I let Ahmed know how astonished I was that while he was gone I hadn't received a cent from the GIA. He was embarrassed. He gave me five thousand dinars "for the kid" and admitted he couldn't give me more because people had stopped supporting the GIA. In a word, racketeering wasn't lucrative anymore and there were fewer and fewer big-time contributors to the cause. Last but not least, I mentioned how ungrateful his friends had been. They showed no concern for me even though they used to come eat at my house every day, and it was largely due to them that I had compromised my health. I thought that especially after the baby was born they'd at least come by to ask how he was doing. It was no use; Ahmed wouldn't acknowledge his friends' failings. He found a way to rationalize their behavior: "They're not as free to move around as they were before. Now they're being hunted down by both the security forces and the people. Their finances are shrinking by the day. They have trouble finding enough to eat. They have to make do with a little *rouina* diluted in water.[1] That's all they have to sustain themselves in the caves where they're hiding out." As he spoke, I could see he was truly unhappy about the adversities his friends were facing.

When I saw how much he was suffering, it made me wish he would die so that he could find peace at last. He rarely experienced happiness, even in his earliest childhood. I looked at him and was angry with myself for having married a man incapable of offering me the tranquility and protection I was seeking. Those were things he never gave me. Tears and arguments, that's all there had been between us. I envied women with no real problems who got to stay home. But it pained me to see him in such a state of filth and degradation. I pleaded with him to turn himself in to the authorities. "I'll only give myself up to God," was his answer. I realized he wasn't interested in human mercy. He wanted to die. He knew the path he'd chosen wasn't leading him anywhere, and he regretted it bitterly. He even admitted it: "I would have liked to have lived with my wife and son. But it's too late now." The fact that he wasn't in control of the village anymore made him feel even worse. Without money or the support of the people, there was nowhere for him to take me. Nothing he could do. He had to desert me and leave me to cope on my own. For someone as cocky as he was, it was the ultimate humiliation, a tremendous disgrace.

Then he pulled himself together and became his old arrogant self again. Despite his weak condition, he was as demanding as ever. He refused the meal my mother prepared for him: it wasn't to his liking. My mother had cooked pumpkin and potato stew. He even went so far as to make fun of it. I reminded him it was his fault that my father had lost his job. I let him know we were thankful to have pumpkin that day because there were some days when all we had was bread and water. He went into the kitchen to make coffee. He insisted on making it himself. He wouldn't eat or drink anything we offered him. The truth is, he didn't trust us. He was afraid we'd put a sleeping pill in his food and call the police. I knew what was going through his mind. Finally, unable to hold back my tears, I told him, "You came back today to make me cry." He retorted angrily, "You always greet me with tears anyway." Any trust there might have been between us was gone. He had totally changed. And so had I.

When we went to bed, he tried to touch me. I pushed him away. The last thing I wanted was to get pregnant again. "You're seeing someone else, aren't you?" he yelled loud enough for the whole household to hear. "I bet it's a cop. Ever since you've been hanging around them, you're completely different!" It wasn't easy to convince him that I had other concerns. He finally calmed down and started talking about children: "I want to have ten or eleven, all terrorists like me." His words made something click in my mind: to him, terrorism was a trade to be passed on from generation to generation. Our son, who was sleeping with us, woke up crying. I turned to breastfeed him. Ahmed let out a shriek that frightened me: "How dare you ignore me to tend to your son? Why didn't you have your mother take him for the night?" I thought to myself, "This is the man who just a few minutes ago told me he wanted a dozen children, and he can't even put up with one." I'm sure Ahmed could have easily done without seeing his son. Yet when he arrived and I put the child in his arms, he was unable to hide his emotion. He even cried. I cried too, but for another reason. I cried because when Ahmed bent over to hug the baby, I saw lice fall from his beard.

I felt he'd also changed in his relationship with me. Before, when he was away for just two or three days, he'd come back burning with desire. This time he approached me less eagerly. He must have married someone else up in the mountains, or he was having sex with other women. Probably with the women they took hostage. It's common practice now. When he and I were married, terrorists didn't do that. If they did take a woman by force, it was to marry her, whether she wanted to or not. They didn't kill women after raping them. I know they took several girls in Haouch Morseli, mostly in the villages around Blida. I think if he felt as strongly about me as he had before, he would have done everything possible to keep me with him. I was willing to follow him anywhere in spite of it all, even up into the mountains. I could have left my son with my mother and gone off with him.

After being away for so long, Ahmed hadn't come back just

to see me and hold his son in his arms. His real purpose was to settle some problems in the village. More specifically, he was supposed to orchestrate the murder of five girls and find the people who had turned his friends in. Four members of the GIA had been killed in Hai Bounab as the result of a tip-off to the police after his departure. Three others managed to get away. The person who had squealed was a former GIA backer. Ahmed also wanted to assess the status of the logistical support networks they usually relied on. Some of those who'd been loyal in the past had stopped providing material aid, and collecting money had become increasingly difficult.

Ahmed asked if anyone had harmed me while he was away. He was all set to execute whoever it was, then and there. I didn't say anything because the first person who caused me hardships after Ahmed left had been my father—by not allowing me to stay in his house and making me beg for shelter from people I hardly knew. There were a few neighbors I could have mentioned, too, but if I got Ahmed worked up about them, he'd have killed them the first chance he got. And besides, people weren't duty bound to take care of me, especially since a lot of them were ignoring me to get even for the extortion my husband had subjected them to.

Ahmed could see for himself that the situation in the village wasn't what it used to be. People who'd staunchly supported the group in the past had changed sides. Now villagers went straight to the police whenever they saw someone they didn't know or anyone who looked the least bit suspicious. That's why not a single terrorist showed his face in Hai Bounab after Ahmed took to the mountains. Ahmed decided he needed to do a clean sweep. But before he did, he had to get me as far away from there as possible, no matter how. When he asked my father to find another place that was nowhere near Hai Bounab, I suspected he was planning to commit atrocities of some sort in the village and was afraid the neighbors might take their revenge out on me. I didn't dare ask what his dark intentions were exactly. But I realized that day to what point he'd lost any semblance of self-restraint. He was now capable of anything, ready to plunge headlong into any danger without thinking, just so it would be over once and for all. He didn't want to admit it, but he was sick of the kind of life he was living. He was eager to die, but he wanted it to be in combat so he'd go to heaven. His death wish had become even stronger following his arm injury and the infections that ensued. For seven months the only thing under the bandages covering his wound was plastic tape. He claimed he'd been treated at the GIA hospital in Djouab, near Medea. They call it a hospital, but I think there's just a nurse there to take care of them.

After that eventful night, he left at dawn, making sure to give me the usual advice: "Be especially careful not to stray from the path of righteousness. Don't betray me. Don't become a traitor." First thing in the morning, my mother went to tell the police about Ahmed's return. They gave her the same advice that Ahmed had given my father: get me out of the village. They were afraid the terrorists would come and abduct me so I could cook their meals for them. Like before.

I never saw Ahmed again.

27

It was back to square one for me. I was happy, though, because the two factions now dominating my life—the police and my husband—had at least given me permission to go wherever I wanted. I felt less constrained. In fact, the police had just stopped requiring me to check in with them every week. My friend Fatma had to continue reporting to the station even after her husband died. But my freedom had a bitter taste. Free to do what? Go where? I had no answers to those questions. Or rather, yes, I did: I was free to go, yet again, in search of some kind soul who might be willing to give me shelter.

Once more, my mother agreed to guide me in my search, a search that was becoming ever more exhausting. It's easier to bear humiliation when you're not alone. She went to Zeralda and pleaded with one of her sisters living with my grandmother to take me in. "You know, the house my sister lives in belongs to my father, so I have some rights to it, too," she said. But my aunt didn't share her point of view and categorically refused to listen. All she had to say was, "I've got eight girls. I don't want them to end up like you." She was afraid my husband's friends would take advantage of my being there to come and kidnap her daughters. She wouldn't even let us spend the night, even though it was already too late to head back to Hai Bounab. My uncle (her brother), who lived next door, was the one who put us up, but under the condition that we be up and out by 6 a.m. I spent the whole night crying. I cried so much that the next morning my eyes were cloudy, as if they were covered by a veil. Regardless, no one took pity on me.

My world had just shrunk a bit more, as it did each time

someone refused to listen to my calls of distress. Perhaps my uncle in Cheraga on my father's side would be more amenable, even though he'd been insensitive to my pain and grief on the last occasion. This time, going to see him was well worth it. But "only for three days, no more." That was because I made a slip-up. I tried to put his wife's mind at ease by telling her Ahmed would come for me as soon as possible. All she could see in her mind was a gang of armed terrorists descending on her house. "Why didn't you tell me that to begin with? I would never have let you set foot in here," she yelled. Luckily, my uncle had already promised my mother I could stay three days. That was the only breather I got.

Then what? For months my parents had followed me as I drifted from place to place like a nomad. They couldn't take it anymore, but they didn't have the heart to desert me. We had already gone to everyone we knew—to no avail. The only option left was to live in the street or commit suicide. Despite everything that had happened, my father still felt some degree of affection for me. He made up his mind to try one more thing: rent a place for my son and me—and for himself, too, since he couldn't bear the thought of leaving me all alone with my baby. He found something in Oued Beni Messous for twenty thousand dinars a year.[1] It depleted his savings—the money he had never wanted to touch. What's more, he had to abandon his wife and children. They stayed in Hai Bounab.

The place was a one-room hovel of cinder blocks and cement, way out in the woods. The doors and windows were nothing but gaping holes. Worse yet, there was no roof, just walls. We took along some sheets of corrugated metal my father had bought to enlarge our house in Hai Bounab and used them to cover all the openings. And of course there was no running water or electricity. The people on the farm next door let us connect a line to their own makeshift wiring. When we needed water, my father would go down to a well a little farther away. Focusing on my son was all I could do to make the time go by in that deserted place. I crocheted while he slept, or made patchwork from old pieces of cloth I'd brought from my mother's. My father was going stir-crazy, so he'd either go to the village or else visit his children. After a few days my mother sent over her one and only television. What great entertainment that was! It helped the time go by a little faster.

The hardest thing to take was seeing my father sink deeper into despair with each passing day. He was lost without his wife there by his side. You could see the distress written all over his face. When he got really depressed, he'd take it out on me. As the days went by, the scenes he made became more frequent and more violent. He blamed me for his situation. "You got married because you wanted to, and against my wishes. But now I'm the one who has to deal with your problems," he kept saying. Sometimes he took it to a higher level: "Since you like the jihad so much, why don't you go off with your husband? Why don't the two of you just drop dead so I can live in peace?"

In the beginning, his outbursts were limited to complaining. Sometimes he raised his voice or shook his fist at me. He even threatened me with a knife, but that was as far as it went. Then one day he exploded. I provoked him because I answered back instead of keeping quiet the way I usually did when he yelled at me. I was just as infuriated as he was. And so, for the first time since I was a child, he beat me. Viciously. I didn't think he had that much brutality in him. Then he left. As soon as I was alone, I dried my tears and began to think: if he beat me like that the first time, he'd kill me for sure if it ever happened again. I was certain he was capable of it. The best thing would be to leave before it was too late. I took my son in my arms and left the house, thinking my father had gone to the village. I had no money or plan, but I was determined not to stay there with him any longer. The forest was thick and I had no idea which way to go to get to the road. I ran, not knowing if I was going in the right direction. I let my instincts guide me and made it almost to the road. I noticed a farm and breathed a sigh of relief. There were other people around. I paused to ask where the bus stop was.

In remote areas like that where you rarely run into anybody, the inhabitants are rather primitive. The sight of strangers makes them apprehensive. When they saw me running with my baby in my arms, they got frightened and started chasing me the way you would a stray dog. My father was at a neighboring farm, less than a hundred yards from there. He knew the owners. He'd worked with them a few years earlier and they'd regularly give him fruit and vegetables. He saw the scene from where he was, and although he probably didn't recognize my face from that distance, he figured that a woman running with a baby in her arms with people chasing after her could only be me. He whistled to get me to turn around. I pretended not to hear, so he started running as fast as he could.

When he caught up with me on the road, he took off my khimar, grabbed me by the hair, and pushed and kicked me in the direction of the house. Then he pulled my son from my arms and threw him into the bushes, shouting in a rage, "You were going back to the terrorists, weren't you? Did they tell you where to meet them?" In tears, I tried to explain that I was only leaving so he could have a normal life again. He wouldn't listen. He hit me in the face and all over my body. The blows came nonstop. My limbs were numb. I was paralyzed and on the verge of passing out. The people from the farm who'd been chasing me a few minutes before took pity on me when they saw me in so much pain, and tried unsuccessfully to intercede. Pulling me by my hair, my father dragged me back to the rented shack. As soon as we got there, he picked up a big stick he found on the ground and beat me. My back was bleeding. I couldn't react anymore and didn't even try to defend myself. I just lay on the ground and let him do what he wanted—to make the job easier for him, so he could finish me off for good! I was expecting to die, convinced he wouldn't stop until he'd killed me.

But I didn't die. Once he had taken all his anger out on me, he fell to the ground like a bag of sand and broke down sobbing: "I left my home and children for you. Everyone has rejected me. They all make fun of me. And you have the nerve to go off and leave me alone." He cried uncontrollably for a long while, then he stopped. In between the spasms of sobs, he made me swear I wasn't planning to go back to join the terrorists. He had a hard time getting the words out. All the sadness of the world shone in his face. Seeing him like that, I felt like my chest was in a vice. I had a lump in my throat. His suffering hurt me terribly—more than the beating he had given me. He looked so unhappy. I threw myself at his feet and begged for forgiveness. That was on November 23, 1996. Two days later I couldn't even get out of bed. I had a fever and was vomiting. Every part of my body was in pain, especially my stomach. My father felt so guilty that he wanted to die. He thought he'd broken my ribs. He went to get the neighbor on the farm nearby who owned a van; he took me to the hospital in Beni Messous. And it was a good thing he did because, in addition to the blows I'd suffered, my infection was flaring up again—it had never been treated properly.

To top it all off, the doctor examining me at the hospital gave me the scare of my life by telling me that, from my symptoms, it seemed I was pregnant. When I heard that, I couldn't hold back any longer. "Now's not the time to have another baby," I yelled. "Do whatever you have to, but I don't want it!" I can't tell you how happy I was when I found out a few days later that my pregnancy test came back negative. But my condition was so bad that the doctors kept me in the hospital for thirteen days. The head of gynecology, Doctor Bouras, took such good care of me that I shared my whole life story with him. He noticed I was a little frightened at first. "Don't worry," he said reassuringly. "We're here to help people. We're not monsters like your husband's friends." Realizing I had no money, he waived some of the fees and personally went to get medication they didn't have on hand at the hospital. He even took care of my son. My mother was looking after him but couldn't afford to buy baby formula, so she gave him regular milk, and he got sick after a week. Not knowing where to turn, she brought him to me in the hospital. Doctor Bouras waited until both my baby and I were completely well before discharging us.

A few days after I got out of the hospital, five girls were murdered in Hai Bounab. Everyone concluded that Ahmed and his friends were behind it. That morning, my mother, along with all my brothers and sisters, came to join us in Oued Beni Messous. She was afraid of reprisals by the victims' families or the patriots. We were packed in that tiny shack for most of what remained of the twelve-month lease, getting along as best we could.

In June 1997, two days after the legislative elections, we made an attempt to return home. My father rented a truck. We piled our belongings into it and even took the corrugated sheet metal we'd brought to block the shack's openings. The whole family was overjoyed that we were finally going home. But when we got to Hai Bounab, we saw our neighbors organizing a demonstration to stop us from moving back into our house. They were all pointing guns at us. Then they marched to the police station to tell them they didn't want us there anymore. "If we let them come back, the terrorists will be back, too," they claimed. And so, despite the police authorization that my father had taken the trouble to get beforehand, we weren't able to move back. The neighbors threatened to burn our truck and lynch us on the spot if we didn't turn around and leave. Their aggressiveness disgusted me. I felt like standing up and reminding them all what short memories they had. There they were, aiming their guns at a helpless family—we were the only ones who weren't armed. Had they so quickly forgotten about the support they'd provided the terrorists themselves? But I didn't want to rile them any more than they were already, so I swallowed my words.

We had no choice but to retrace our steps with all our belongings and sheet metal. Fortunately, we had two more months left on our lease. We blocked up the shack's openings again. The neighbor on the farm next door saw us returning at dusk. She felt sorry for us and offered to let us stay at her place. That night my father took his anger out on me once again. It had become a ritual, and I'd learned to expect it. Ever since that first beating he gave me, it was an almost daily event. And this time one of my brothers helped him. All my brothers and sisters approved. They were so disappointed over not being able to go back home that they made me pay the price. I'll never forget the beating I got.

28

All the villagers in Hai Bounab supported the terrorists. It used to be that they were overjoyed whenever a policeman or patriot got killed. They assumed anyone who was in any way tied to the government had to be rich and powerful. But when the GIA started massacring civilians, including people who had nothing to do with the government at either the national or local levels, and especially after they began indiscriminately slaughtering entire families, the empathy the people felt for the movement turned to horror. The truth is, when the people realized no one was safe from the GIA's killing frenzy, they reevaluated their position. As was the case elsewhere, in Hai Bounab the mobilization against the GIA was just as strong and sudden as had been the support for it. Probably even more so, since there were fewer young people joining the GIA than taking up the cause against it. There's not a single house in the village that doesn't have a weapon. The people in Hai Bounab changed sides the day the five girls were beheaded. That's when they realized that the same thing could happen to them. A week earlier a list was found in a house that the terrorists had occupied; it identified the people they planned to kill. Almost half the villagers' names were on it — everyone whose support for the GIA had become lax. Following the discovery, the police offered the people weapons and warned them that a massacre might be on the way. At first the villagers thought it was a trap. "After everything we've done for them, the GIA wouldn't hurt us," they said with unwavering conviction.

Then the five girls were decapitated and their heads thrown in front of the doors of people on the list. It was a message. I knew those girls would be the first victims. When Ahmed came back after being away for seven months, he asked me about Saloua, her three sisters, and one of their friends, Fatiha. Saloua and Fatiha were good friends of mine. I was certain Ahmed and his group were planning to do something to them. That same day, he admitted that he and his brothers had committed the massacre in Benramdane a few months earlier. They had killed the men there because they had volunteered to take up arms against the GIA. They had killed the girls because they went out too often, wore short dresses, and were the only women in the village who didn't wear a hijab. The GIA also didn't like the fact that the girls worked. They'd been warned but didn't want to give up their jobs. It was their means of supporting themselves and their families. I think Ahmed and his group started with the girls out of cowardice. They knew the other neighbors didn't much care for the girls either because of the freedom they displayed in their behavior. They hung around men and opened their windows—something that was forbidden in Hai Bounab. Since the neighbors had banded together against the girls, the terrorists thought the people would approve of the slaughter. But although the neighbors might have considered the girls debauched, they certainly didn't want to see them die. It was a brutal shock to everyone in Hai Bounab.

The people in the village had been so spineless in other instances that the terrorists never imagined they would one day turn against them. A month before the girls were murdered, an incident occurred involving Saloua's father that illustrated the villagers' complete lack of backbone. At the time, all the residents had to lock their doors at 6 p.m. Regardless of what might happen during the night, they couldn't open their doors until morning. That was the rule the GIA had imposed. One evening around ten o'clock, the girls' father, who had a heart condition, suffered a severe attack. The girls began screaming and went knocking door-to-door, trying to get somebody to help take him to the hospital. None of the villagers opened their doors. My father was the only one who went outside, but it wasn't out of courage. That night, he was sleeping at the house next door. The men had started grouping together at a different neighbor's house each night so they'd be in a better position to fend off any potential assaults. When my father heard the screaming, he thought it was me—that the police had come to take me away. He went outside in his shorts and came face to face with the girls. They were in tears. He couldn't wiggle out of the situation, so he went to help their father, massaged his chest, and got him breathing again. The next day my father told me that if he'd known what all the noise was about, he wouldn't have bothered to go outside. And the height of hypocrisy was that those same neighbors who wouldn't open their doors to help that poor man later went to ask how he was doing. Plus, they openly acknowledged to the girls that they thought the terrorists were slitting their throats. Their cynicism was too much for Saloua, the oldest. She went into a blind rage. "You're a bunch of cowards," she told them bluntly. "And now you pretend to be concerned about my father's health? What if they really do come to kill us? Will you do anything to stop them?" The neighbors were unanimous: "You're on your own, like everyone else." Saloua couldn't restrain herself. She kicked them all out of the house. Fatiha was aware that she was a target. More than once she told me: "They're going to kill Saloua and me for sure." When I asked her why she was so certain, she didn't answer. I found out later she was frightened because she was going out with a patriot.

A month after that incident, the girls were killed. The terrorists made them go outside in the middle of the night. They were screaming like madwomen. The whole village heard them yelling, but no one lifted a finger. Hafida, the youngest of Saloua's sisters, was shot in the head in her bed because she fainted when they tried to get her to go outside. She was such a nice person. She and my brother were dating and had planned to get married. She was seventeen. My mother was in Hai Bounab that day and saw Ahmed. She left the village the next day, as did all the neighbors. The sight of the heads at the doorsteps of the houses had instilled terror in everyone. The residents didn't return until they had been supplied with guns to confront those who had now become their common enemies.

The incident shows how incredibly easy it is for people to change with the tide. The residents of Hai Bounab knew everything the terrorists were doing. The ones who didn't help them directly were accomplices by virtue of their silence. The day my parents and I returned to our house and I saw them all threatening my family with their guns, I wanted to yell in their faces, "How come you never said anything all those times you saw me leave with the group at five in the morning? Why didn't you call the police when your children stood watch for them and ran errands for me so I could cook their meals?" Back then they were too chicken-hearted to take action. Either that or they supported it. I can understand why they were like that, though. They'd been paralyzed by the atrocities that they knew the GIA had committed. I remember that a woman had said something bad about me once. She was someone who liked to talk a lot. She'd spread a rumor in the neighborhood that I'd had a child by another man before I was married. Ahmed got wind of it and without giving it a second thought went to her house to slit her throat. Fortunately she wasn't there. Her husband came out and managed to appease Ahmed's anger by pleading with him on his knees. Her husband had always been nice to Ahmed when he was younger, and Ahmed respected him. That's the only reason he didn't kill her. But I'm certain that if she'd been home, nothing would have stopped him.

It was that kind of abusive cruelty that turned all their former allies against them. Take my brother for example. The one who is fifteen. He adored Ahmed and his friends. Idolized them.

Now they make him sick. In fact, he was the one who tipped off the police about the group in Bouchaoui the last time.[1] He used to go to work sites once in a while with a friend and collect unused copper piping then sell it to people driving by on the highway to make a little spending money. One day while he was crossing through an orchard he heard someone moaning. He walked toward the sounds and found an old man who'd been struck on the head with a pickax. He ran to alert the orchard's caretaker, but the caretaker was too afraid to report it to the police. He sent my brother to inform the victim's son, who was a patriot. Following the incident, there was a thorough search of the area and several terrorists were killed. The most astonishing part was seeing how happy my brother was to have been the one to bring it to the attention of the patriots.

Nothing would have given my father greater pleasure than strangling Ahmed with his bare hands. He had asked for a gun, but the police refused to give him one so long as his son-in-law was still alive. He tried to convince them that he was the only one who could track Ahmed down because he knew how my husband operated. He's glad he owns a shotgun now. Just like all the residents of Hai Bounab. But he won't have to use it to kill Ahmed. I was obsessed for a long time by the thought that my father would kill my husband. How would my son have reacted later in life if he learned that his grandfather had murdered his father?

29

In August 1997 my family went to my uncle's in Cheraga. All twelve of us. We didn't have the money to renew the lease on the place in Oued Beni Messous. This time, my uncle didn't dare send us away. We stayed for more than a year, but he certainly didn't make life easy for us. On the contrary, he never missed an opportunity to let us know we were in the way. It was an unpleasant situation for him, too. He had to stop construction on his house to put us up in two cinder block rooms he was building. He was anxious to complete the work but couldn't so long as we were there. The first thing he asked me the day we arrived was whether or not I had brought any money. He thought perhaps the Hai Bounab terrorist cell's money was still at my house. My father had asked me the same question. It's obvious that if I'd had money I would have been treated differently.

I have another uncle who lives in Cheraga, not far from the first. He owns a three-story house, but he would never let us stay there, even for one night. He was afraid of the neighbors' reactions. They all knew my husband was a GIA emir because some of the people in Hai Bounab have relatives in Cheraga and they talk to each other regularly. And besides, everybody knows everybody else's business. For example, one day I unexpectedly ran into a former classmate I hadn't seen in eight years. I pretended not to recognize her because I didn't want to subject myself to the questions I knew she'd ask. But she recognized me and stopped to talk. She already knew every detail of my life and claimed that all my other girlfriends did, too. That uncle with the big house has done pretty well for himself financially, and he knew that letting us stay there would be bad for his business. On the few occasions when we visited him—for traditional holidays—his neighbors always made their children go inside when they saw us coming and slammed their doors and windows shut to avoid having to say hello to us. They said we smelled like terrorists.

The whole time we were in Cheraga, we had to keep to ourselves and not draw anyone's attention. One of my brothers is handicapped, and the kids in the neighborhood used to gang up on him and yell insults, but we didn't do anything about it. We put up with everything and never said a word. Especially me. It was the price we had to pay to have a roof over our heads—a privilege that had not come easily and that could be taken away at any moment. My uncle was mean to my son. On more than one occasion I caught him hitting the baby and trying to turn my little brothers against him. He'd pull food out of the child's mouth and go into a rage if he saw anyone feeding him. "You're fattening up the son of a terrorist so he'll grow up and be just like his father," he used to say. He didn't dare confront me directly because he assumed I was still in contact with my husband. He took it out on my son instead.

The thing that hurt me most was seeing the predicament my sisters were in. They were throwing away their futures, and it was because of me. Faouzia, who is twelve and was always at the head of her class, had to stop going to school for two years. They wouldn't let her enroll in Cheraga because she wasn't a resident of the town. My uncle refused to apply for a certificate of residence for us because he was afraid we'd never leave if he did. But there was more to it than that. The school officials were wary of us and suspected we were up to something. My other sister, Shahrazed, who is nine, was in the same situation.

Besides that, our financial resources were extremely limited. My nineteen-year-old brother was the only one with a job. He worked on construction sites. He didn't speak to me for six years after I started seeing Ahmed. He never said hello to me, and I wasn't allowed to touch anything that belonged to him when he was around. I couldn't even make his bed or put his clothes away. If he knew I had prepared the meal, he refused to eat it. And like my uncle, he didn't want to see anyone feeding my son. He didn't want the money he brought home to be used to help "raise the son of a terrorist." He even went so far as to forbid me to use the detergent he bought to wash my son's things.

My other brother is seventeen. He's worse than the older one. He helps my uncle out at his barbershop and earns just enough to cover the cost of cigarettes and other small expenses. On the feast day of Aïd, my father took my son to my uncle's shop to get his hair cut. They made them hang around the whole day then refused to wait on them. After he started walking, the cement pavement in the yard hurt his feet. No one ever offered to buy him a pair of shoes. He went an entire year without any. Yet my uncle isn't bad off. Besides owning the barbershop, he deals in spare auto parts. He does all right for himself.

My third brother is fifteen. He quit school before we left Hai Bounab. He didn't like to study. Even when he was little, he used to play hooky. My eleven-year-old brother is the handicapped one; he has a motor disability. We'd love to be able to place him in a specialized care center, but you need connections for that. And I have two little sisters, aged four and seven. If my mother hadn't lost a baby girl in childbirth, there would be ten of us.

My mother-in-law can afford to help her grandson, but she doesn't. She's never even tried to see him. Yet when I was pregnant, she used to say: "If it's a boy, I'll take good care of him." I could make trouble for her if I wanted by letting it be known that it was my husband who bought her everything she owns: the house, the cows, the van, the grocery store, et cetera, and that he put everything in his older brother's name. The police chief guaranteed me he'd help fight for what was mine if I wanted. But my mother-in-law's plight pains me. The suffering she's endured from the loss of her three sons is bad enough. I don't want to add to it. And besides, she's pretty crafty. A few months ago she sold everything, bought a house in another town with her youngest son, and put the rest of the money in the bank.

To get out of the rut I was in, I needed to find a safe place to stay so my family could go back home. But there aren't many people willing to take in the wife of a terrorist, even if he's dead. In desperation, I went to community centers for the poor, but they were already overcrowded. I talked to a lot of people, hoping one of them might help me find a solution, but no one could do anything for me. Then one day while I was watching TV, I saw Dalila. She is the president of an association that helps needy women. She was explaining about the services they offer. "She's the one who'll get me out of this," I immediately thought. I called the number she'd given on TV and got the association's address. I went to see her and poured out my entire story. I held nothing back. She helped me financially right away—and my family, too. Then she arranged for me to stay with a family she knew. It worked out really well. I'm still with them today.

30

Now that Ahmed is dead, I feel like I'm coming back to life. When we got married, all I wanted was a quiet existence. We would most likely have lived in poverty, and I would have had to make do with "the earth for my bed and the sky for a blanket," as Ahmed used to say when he was in a romantic mood before we got married. How could I have imagined back then that he would be bringing me the clothes and furnishings of the people he murdered?

I hope my story can serve as an example for other young women. I got into this mess because I was in love with a man who, all things considered, I hardly knew. We lived together for only three months. I'll tell my son everything as soon as he's old enough to understand. He has to know the truth some day.

My friend Fatma found peace once again, too, after the death of her husband. Her brothers had rejected her when she got married, but they've since come around and are taking good care of her daughter. Fatma is going to remarry—this time she is marrying a man who has nothing to do with terrorism. The only problem is that her daughter's name still doesn't appear on any public records. When they do register her birth, she will have to be listed as "born to an unwed mother and unknown father." Fatma's mother-in-law has sworn that the little girl is in fact her son's daughter, but that hasn't satisfied the administrative officials.

The hardships I've been through have caused me to doubt everything, even religion. I continued to say my prayers for a while after my husband died, but not diligently. I didn't say them on cold mornings because it would have meant getting up early and going out into the yard to do my ablutions. Now I've stopped completely. My father is like me. He says a prayer every once in a while to ask God to help him with something. As for my mother, she never prayed. So now I have to ask myself, "Does God favor people like Ahmed who never miss saying their prayers but who kill innocent victims?" When I think of everything I've endured, I figure, "Why should I pray to God anymore after what he has put me through?" He never listened to my prayers anyway. I've stopped doing the things my husband told me I needed to do if I wanted to go heaven, like keeping my hijab on in the house, even in front of my mother and father. I don't wear a niqab anymore when I go out. And I've even been going outside without my hijab lately. The other day I went to the hairdresser's and got my hair cut, and I wear tights around the house. I couldn't do any of those things before.

I've been very happy since I moved in with this family. "You'll be just like my own daughter," the woman of the house told me on my first day here. I do the housework for them in exchange for room and board. My room is heated and comfortable. It had been a long time since I had my own room. Actually, I never did. My parents are very pleased, too. When I left, it meant their hardship and humiliation had come to an end. They moved back into their house in Hai Bounab. They don't have a lot of money, but they're happy.

My only desire now is to be able to get my son back one day. I had to leave him with my mother.

Algiers
February 1998

NOTES

CHAPTER 1

1. Chrea: A mountain chain overlooking the fertile Mitidja Plain surrounding Algiers. Once a vacation spot, it has become a GIA stronghold.
2. Emir: "Leader" in Arabic. Title given to leaders of armed Islamist groups. There is an emir for each locality. They are all under the authority of a countrywide emir.
3. The family record book is a legal document given to the husband on his wedding day. Births, deaths and any changes in marital status must be entered in it by civil officials. —Trans.
4. The communal guard: A supplemental backup for the army, created to defend the villages against terrorism. It replaced the local guard, which was disbanded in 1982.

CHAPTER 2

1. President Boumedienne (1965–78) made agriculture one of the priorities of his Socialist policy and gave special consideration to farmers working on land that had once belonged to colonists.
2. Farming estates were created from the farms left vacant following the departure of the French colonists and were entirely government-owned.
3. In 1987 the government estates were reorganized into EACs (collective farming enterprises) or EAIs (individual farming enterprises). By law, groups of farmhands could work the land and retain the usufruct.
4. US$1 = approximately DA70.

CHAPTER 3

1. Mulud: Birthday of the prophet Muhammad, a popular holiday.

CHAPTER 4

1. Bougara: Formerly Rovigo, a town in the district of Blida in the Mitidja region and one of the GIA's first strongholds.
2. Patriots: A legitimate defense group. A corps comprised of civilians, replacing the army, created to defend the villages against terrorists.

CHAPTER 5

1. Located just less than two miles east of Algiers, Setif has long been known as a hub for contraband goods.

CHAPTER 6

1. Cheb Hasni was an immensely popular raï singer who was assassinated by the GIA in Oran in 1995.
2. Your absence, my love, has lasted too long.

CHAPTER 7

1. *Khimar*: Scarf used by Muslim women to cover their heads.
2. *Taghout*: Tyrant. Term used by Islamists to refer to members of the government, and, by extension, anyone who is not on their side.
3. Age of ignorance: The pre-Islamic period, according to Muslim belief.
4. "Group": Term Ahmed always used to refer to the Armed Islamic Group to which he belonged, first as a member and later as its emir.
5. In many regions, especially rural areas, even non-Islamist women put on headscarves to go out, but remove them indoors, contrary to militant Islamists who keep their scarves on at all times.
6. *Kamis*: Long robe worn by male Islamists. *Siwak*: Walnut tree bark used by Islamists for whitening teeth, as in the time of the prophet Muhammad.
7. *Dhor*: The prayer said in the early afternoon.
8. *Asr*: Mid-afternoon prayer.
9. In regions where water is scarce, it is permitted to perform ablutions with a stone, since the essential element is the symbolism of washing. Permission to do so has been extended to the ailing. Others who claim to be muftis can also grant it if they so desire.

CHAPTER 8

1. "Mother of the faithful": Title given to Khadidja, the prophet's first wife, who was the first to embrace the Muslim religion. Islamists give the title to their emirs' wives.
2. Caliphate—Political dominion under the leadership of those claiming succession from Muhammad.—Trans.
3. *Mujahideen*—One who wages a holy war.—Trans.
4. *Mahchoucha*: Sawed-off shotgun. The weapon is commonly used by terrorist groups in Algeria.

CHAPTER 9

1. *Mhadjeb*: A thin oily crust stuffed with onion, tomato, garlic, and hot pepper.
   Rfis: A mixture of grilled, coarse semolina, butter, and crushed dates.
   Tamina: The same recipe as for *rfis*, but using honey instead of crushed dates.
   Khouchkhach: Cakes made with a thinly rolled crust fried in oil, then soaked in honey.
   Maarek: A thin oily crust baked on a metal tray and soaked in honey.
2. *Chakchouka*: A salad composed mainly of grilled, peeled tomatoes and peppers, seasoned with olive oil.
3. *Chorba*: A soup with a vegetable, meat, and tomato base.
   Bourek: A type of pancake stuffed with meat.
4. *Djelbab*: A wide, floor-length black veil worn low over the forehead, covering the wearer's eyes.

CHAPTER 10

1. *Fitna*: Discord, unrest.
2. Muhammad Boudiaf: President of Algeria from January to June 1992. He was assassinated by a member of his personal guard.
3. The *caïd*, or boss, is the local emir's right-hand man.—Trans.

CHAPTER 12

1. *Jihad*: Holy war.

2. Radio Koran: A public Algerian radio station that broadcasts only sacred texts and religious songs.

3. Abdallah Djaballah: President of an Islamist opposition party with representation in Parliament.

4. *Sunna*: Traditional literature recounting the words and acts of Muhammad.

5. Mahfoud Nahnah: President of the MSP (Movement for a Peaceful Society, formerly Hamas), an Islamist party belonging to the government coalition (Nahnah died on July 2, 2003—Trans.).

6. Abassi Madani: President of the FIS (Islamic Salvation Front), disbanded in March 1992.

CHAPTER 13

1. At the time, Antar Zouabri was just the "regional emir." He became the "national emir" in July, 1996.

2. Antar Zouabri was killed by security forces in February, 2002. He was 32 years old.—Trans.

3. Douar Lahdjar: A small village on the Mitidja Plain, near Boufarik. It was a terrorist stronghold where hideouts and bomb-making laboratories were based.

Ouled Allel: A small village near Baraki that was deserted by its inhabitants and taken over by the GIA. The army carried out an extensive search operation there in the summer of 1997.

4. *Falaqa*: A beating administered with a stick or whip, often on the soles of the feet. The method of punishment is widespread among Islamists.

5. *Hosn El Muslim*: A book of instructions on behavior to be followed by good Muslims, widely read by fundamentalists.

6. Islamists use a specific language that draws much of its vocabulary from ancient Arabic and theological terminology.

CHAPTER 15

1. *Fatwa*: A legal notice given by Muslim scholars. Members of the GIA, however, draw up their own fatwas.

CHAPTER 16

1. *Bouchouour*: "The man with thick hair."

2. Although, strictly speaking, *hijab* refers to the practice of dressing modestly, the term is often used to refer to a headscarf. —Trans.

CHAPTER 18

1. *Niqab*: A small veil Islamist women wear over the face and that sometimes covers the eyes.

CHAPTER 20

1. *Khalti*: Aunt in Arabic. A colloquial term sometimes used to designate older woman.
Chlef: A town 160 miles west of Algiers.
2. *Derbouka*: A percussion instrument made of a ceramic drum covered at the base with fish skin or goat hide.

CHAPTER 21

1. *Rahma*: Clemency. The Rahma law was enacted in 1995 and is applied to terrorists who have renounced terrorism. They receive lighter sentences, especially if they agree to collaborate with the security forces.

CHAPTER 26

1. *Rouina*: Flour made of grilled wheat.

CHAPTER 27

1. Oued Beni Messous: A small remote village about twelve miles west of Algiers. Several large massacres took place there during the summer of 1997.

CHAPTER 28

1. This GIA group was gunned down in the forest of Bouchaoui, nine miles outside of Algiers, in the fall of 1997.